I'm Proud of You

My Friendship
With Fred Rogers

Tim Madigan

Praise for I'm Proud of You

"A loving testament to the power of friendship and to a most remarkable man. Goodbye, Fred, we'll miss you. And thank you for this book."—*The Boston Sunday Globe*

"Deeply moving. . . ."—*Library Journal*

Fred inspired because he saw the good in everyone, Fred challenged because he wanted everyone to see the good in themselves. Now Fred comes to life in *I'm Proud of You*, with his simple goodness etched on every page, and his complicated greatness etched in the heart of every reader who finishes the book and decides to become a better person."—Tom Junod, writer at large for *Esquire*

"*I'm Proud of You* is a beautiful book...For fans of Mister Rogers or those seeking a quiet, uplifting read, *I'm Proud of You* is an absolute treasure."—*BookPage*

I'm Proud of You

Ubuntu Press, Los Angeles

Copyright © 2012 by Tim Madigan

For LaMoure J. "Myke" Madigan, with much love and gratitude.
IPOY, too, Dad

Chapter 1

On a sunny Sunday afternoon, in that bleak season of 1997, I knelt in the front yard of my suburban Texas home, in a mood anything but festive, trying to arrange Christmas lights. Inside that home, my marriage was falling apart. I knew these might be the last holidays I would ever spend in this home, with this family. And as I worked, my mind raced with questions, all of them painful.

When would Catherine and I break the news to our two children—Melanie, who had just turned eighteen, and six-year-old Patrick? What words could we possibly use to soften the blow? Should we wait until after the holidays to tell them? Could we hold it together until then? What would my parents and Catherine's family think when they heard? How much could I afford to pay for an apartment? Where would I find furniture?

There was also this question that day, one that caused as much shame and dread in me as the rest. How could I possibly tell my famous friend in Pittsburgh, Fred Rogers, the gentle icon of public television's Mister Rogers' Neighborhood, that my wife and I were about to split up?

It seemed such a wildly unlikely predicament then, having to share that news with Fred. It still seems remarkable today that he and I would have known each other at all. But I had indeed met him, traveling from Texas to Pittsburgh two years before to profile Mister Rogers for my newspaper, the *Fort Worth Star-Telegram*, then embracing his surprising invitation to friendship.

Looking back, it seems no coincidence that our unlikely acquaintance would come when it did, in the darkest, most difficult period of my life—five years or so when I wrestled with profound depression and self-loathing, complex and painful feelings about my father (Fred called these various struggles my "Furies"), and finally, the catastrophic illness and heroic spiritual journey of my younger brother, Steve. In any event, within a few months of our meeting in the fall of 1995, in a series of e-mail messages and telephone calls, and in several visits to Pittsburgh, I began to share with Fred the tattered state of my insides.

Each time I did, he responded with what can only be described as supernatural love, wholly without judgment, and with perfect clarity, wisdom, and compassion. "Anything mentionable is manageable," he would say, inviting me to share further. Or he would paraphrase his good friend, the Roman Catholic priest and celebrated author Henri Nouwen, by saying, "That which is most personal is most universal." As I poured out my heart to Fred, beginning in those early days of our friendship, it began to seem like I was testing him, searching for a foible, for something I could say or do that would finally render him incapable of unconditional regard.

And on that sunny December afternoon in 1997, I was sure I had finally found it. He was a man who had devoted his life to children and their families, and I was a man about to destroy his own. After the lights were finished, I finally summoned my nerve, went inside to our computer, and typed out a letter to my friend, tears of remorse streaming down my cheeks. After years of counseling and struggle, my marriage was probably ending and I was the one ending it, I told Mister Rogers in my letter that day. Could he forgive such a person? Could he continue to love such a man?

His reply arrived within the week, dated December 20, 1997, two full pages on the stationery of Mister Rogers' Neighborhood, written in Fred's pinched, meticulous, highly distinctive hand. I did not make it through the first paragraph before I again began to cry.

My dear Tim,

Bless your heart. I feel so for you—for you all—but, Tim, please know that I would never forsake you, that I will never be disappointed with you, that I would never stop loving you. How I wish we could be closer geographically! I'd get in my car, drive to your house, knock on your door, and, when you answered I'd hug you tight.

You are a beautiful man, inside and out, and those who care about you are privileged to share your pain . . . As for suffering: I believe that there are fewer people than ever who escape major suffering in this life. In fact I'm fairly convinced that the Kingdom of God is for the broken-hearted. You write of "powerlessness." Join the club, we are not in control: God is.

Our trust and affection run very deep. You know you are in my prayers—now and always. If you ever need me you have only to call and I would do my best to get to you, or you to me . . .

. . . You are my beloved brother, Tim. You are God's beloved son.

On February 28, 2003, the day after Fred's death from stomach cancer at age seventy-four, I published an essay in the *Star-Telegram* describing our unlikely friendship. For the next several days I was inundated with hundreds of letters, e-mails, and telephone messages from newspaper readers eager to share their own memories of Mister Rogers, and the impact he and his long-running children's program had on their lives. Scores of young adults wrote of the sense of security they felt growing up with him, of learning from Mister Rogers about their own value and what it meant to love. Parents wrote of entrusting their children to Mister Rogers for a half hour each day, the kindly, wise, civilizing influence in a world increasingly bereft of kindness, wisdom, and civility.

As I answered those messages, I was pleased to assure the readers that Fred Rogers and Mister Rogers were indeed one and the same, that in real life Fred was as he appeared on television, the gentle embodiment of goodness and grace.

But I also told them that, in my opinion, Mister Rogers' Neighborhood revealed only a fraction of his human greatness. Knowing him from television alone, it was tempting to see him as a man who might actually live in his Neighborhood of Make Believe (a popular puppet segment of his show), a person of epic goodness, no doubt, but also a man of innocence and naiveté, who, as a result, might be little acquainted with the grittier realities of life (though his program dealt unflinchingly with issues like divorce, death, and violence). It was that seeming innocence that made Mister Rogers such an inviting target for satire. (Fred once told me of surprising Eddie Murphy at his dressing room for Saturday Night Live, the comedy where Murphy repeatedly spoofed Fred in sketches called Mister Robinson's Neighborhood. Eddie Murphy's television neighborhood was a raunchy place populated by slumlords, pimps, and prostitutes. "Oh, my God," Murphy cried when he saw Fred that day. 'The real Mister Robinson!" And, of course, the two hugged.)

There was innocence about Fred in person, to be sure. He could be quaint, such as when he referred to me as "my dear." He was a vegetarian who would never eat "anything that had a mother." He wore a goofy-looking swimming cap and goggles for his daily morning swims. He forever carried a camera, pulling it out with great delight to photograph people he had met for the first time.

But he was also a man fully of this world, deeply aware of and engaged in its difficulties, speaking often of death, disease, divorce, addiction, and cruelty and the agonies those things wrought on people he loved. He worked very hard, a life-long student of children and child development who agonized over each word and gesture in Mister Rogers' Neighborhood. ("I feel such a responsibility to do my best for the children," he told me once before he sat down to tackle a new script.) He was a firm taskmaster on the Mister Rogers set, especially if things were not quite to his satisfaction. An ordained Presbyterian minister, he devoured books by the great spiritual writers and was constantly preoccupied with spiritual questions himself. He rose before six each morning to pray for dozens of people by name. He was perhaps the most intelligent person I've ever known.

But in my mind, something else was at the heart of his greatness. It was his unique capacity for relationship, what *Esquire* magazine writer Tom Junod once called "a fearlessness, an unashamed insistence on intimacy." That was true with almost every person he met, be it television's Katie Couric or a New York City cabdriver, the Dalai Lama or the fellow handing out towels at the health club where Fred went to swim. Fred wanted to know the truth of your life, the nature of your insides, and had room enough in his own spirit to embrace without judgment whatever that truth might be.

Even mine.

"Your wounded heart is a very beautiful heart," Fred wrote to me once in the midst of the Furies. "In fact, it has probably allowed you to understand the hearts of all others who are wounded.' And whose isn't, in some way? Some are just a little more obvious than others. Please know that I think of you and pray for you every day . . . yes, every day. You've touched a very deep part of my being too, you know ... I'm grateful to God for you."

On April 3, 1998, after again reaching out to him when the world looked bleak, I received this e-mail message at my newspaper desk.

"Even if you can't believe in your own goodness from time to time, please know that I always do," Fred wrote. "You are a superb person. I feel constantly blessed to be able to call you my 'Anam Cara.' (Gaelic for 'spiritual friend.')"

Among the dozens of e-mails I received from him over the years was one in which Fred wrote that I had "allowed myself to be blessed" by sharing my pain.

"Of course, those of us with whom you have shared are all the richer because you've allowed us to walk in your inner garden," he wrote then. "And what a glorious garden it is!"

Another time he wrote that he had discovered the South African word ubuntu, which means: I am because we are. "Isn't that lovely!" he said. "My identity is such that it includes you. I would be a very different person without you."

I woke up one morning in 1998 to find another e-mail in which Fred quoted a prayer by a minister named Harry Emerson Fosdick. "We confess before Thee that if life were all smooth, there would be no patience; were it all easy, no courage, no sacrifice, no depth of character. We acknowledge before Thee that what is most admirable is the child of adversity and of courageous souls unafraid to face it."

Fred concluded that note by saying, "of course, I think of you often, but just wanted you to have this before I go to sleep tonight."

Thus, with those words, and in dozens of other letters, e-mails, and telephone conversations, and in several visits to his home over the years, Fred Rogers guided me through the Furies, the loving witness to my often-difficult journey. "Please know that I would never forsake you," he had written. I still marvel that in that time of personal hell, I had been blessed by the human embodiment of heaven.

Catherine and I made it through Christmas in 1997, and put off telling the kids about the looming separation. Even in our most difficult times, my wife and I were kind and respectful toward each other, and that holiday season was no different. So on the surface, at least, there was peace in our house. In a Christmas Eve entry from my journal, I wrote of seeing my young son that morning, dressed in dinosaur pajamas, the picture of security and contentment. "As completely strange as it seems, we had the most fun Christmas Eve that I can remember," I wrote on Christmas Day. "Patrick was so excited. Melanie's [friends] came over and we all laughed so much."

Just before New Year's, I left by myself for the mountains of New Mexico for several days of reading, writing, and much praying and soul-searching. As is often the case with me, time alone in the brisk mountain air brought healing and clarity. It was then that I realized (once again) that I had mistakenly blamed my wife for my own old wounds. The real issue was not Catherine, or our marriage, but the man looking back at me in the mirror, and I managed to convince my wife of that when I returned to Texas.

Which led to Fred's next letter, dated January 14, 1998.

My dear Tim,

Your letter greeted me when I got in last night: "Catherine and I are not going to separate," I read, and my heart jumped, and my lips said, "Thank God." You've been through so much together and you're continuing to grow in such important ways: I rejoice for both of you—and of course for Patrick and Melanie.

I hope someday you'll know—deep down—how important it is for me to have such a trusting and trustworthy friend. As you probably do know: I pray for you and thank God for you every day. My love is with you always.

Three months later, on March 20, we sent Fred a candle for his seventieth birthday. "I'm glad we were both born in the same century," he told me when I called him that day. He said he was also touched that all four of us had signed his birthday card "after all that we've been through."

Today, Catherine and I are the happiest married couple we know. She is the love and anchor of my life, the last voice I hear every night, and the person with whom I share my heart over the first cup of coffee every morning. Our house is a place of happiness and peace. The Furies are an increasingly distant memory. But with Fred as my friend, I wonder how it could have been otherwise. What demons could withstand such a perfectly and consistently loving assault?

Chapter 2

To be honest, I was a Captain Kangaroo kid. The Captain and his friends on that wonderful children's program—Mr. Green Jeans, Bunny Rabbit, Mr. Moose, and the rest—were as much a part of my boyhood mornings as bowls of Cheerios and walking to school through the Minnesota snow. A timid, dreamy boy, I liked it that the Captain's world was a gentle place where life moved slowly, except when Mr. Moose caused Ping-Pong balls to rain on Captain Kangaroo's head.

Mister Rogers' Neighborhood came along on public television in 1968, when I was eleven, somewhat past the age of that program's target audience. Years later, my own children would regularly tune in to Fred, but by the autumn of 1995 I had watched the show no more than a half-dozen times myself, and then only in snatches, between gulps of morning coffee. I am not proud to say that I was more familiar with Eddie Murphy's raunchy parody of Mister Rogers on Saturday Night Live than I was with Mister Rogers' Neighborhood itself.

So when I prepared to interview the two children's television icons in October 1995, the idea of speaking to Bob Keeshan (Captain Kangaroo) excited me most. At the time, I was reporting a story about violence on television and its effect on children, and had submitted interview requests with the public relations assistants of the two men. Captain Kangaroo and Mister Rogers actually got back to me on the same day, within an hour of each other. How many newspaper reporters can say that?

Keeshan called first, telling me that he and Fred, both then in their late sixties, were actually good friends and made a point of speaking on the telephone every New Year's Day. I found Captain Kangaroo to be a kindly, thoughtful man greatly concerned by the vulgar and violent images increasingly bombarding children on television. But our talk was relatively brief. Then, a few minutes after we hung up, my phone rang again, and for the first time other than on television, I heard that voice, speaking as softly and slowly to me on the telephone as he did to his young viewers each morning.

Fred and I talked for almost an hour. He told me then of visiting his parents' home in Latrobe, Pennsylvania, shortly after graduating from college in 1951, and seeing on their new television what passed for children's programming, "which included a lot of throwing pies in each other's faces." Somehow he figured he could do better, that children deserved more.

"I decided I'd like to try my hand at this new medium," he said. "It wasn't hard to deduce that if this picture and sound were in everybody's living room, it could have a wonderfully positive influence."

Thus were the origins of one of America's most cherished rituals: Mister Rogers bursting happily though the door of his television home singing "Won't You Be My Neighbor?" From a closet came the famous cardigan sweater with a zipper in front (a red one now resides in the Smithsonian) first knitted for him by his mother. Grown-up shoes were replaced by a pair of blue boating sneakers as the television host settled in to give children his undivided attention.

"Our program has a built-in surrogate parent," Fred told me on the telephone that first day. "What is presented is filtered through this concerned adult. Most programs simply present stuff with absolutely nobody to have a helpful arm around the child.

"All the better if you have a live person there with an arm around you," he continued. "But if you don't, you should have somebody there to say, 'This is just pretend.' It all depends on how much we care about children. Is it realistic to think that we care enough about our children to put them first? It isn't that we don't know what can be helpful. That's not an excuse. We know the kinds of models that are healthy to give to children. And that doesn't mean they are dull."

As that surrogate adult, Fred said, he quite literally tried to look through the camera into the eyes of each child watching, speaking to them as if individually, trying to be fully present to their feelings and needs. But then, he said, that was important when people of any age came together—no matter who they were or under what circumstances. For instance:

"Do you know the most important thing in the world to me right now?" Fred asked me that day.

No, I said.

"Talking to Mr. Tim Madigan on the telephone."

I'm sure I blushed, incredulous and skeptical. But somehow, in the way he said it, in that famous, gentle, oh-so-slow voice, I knew that the famous man was speaking the truth.

The November day a few weeks later was crisp and clear as I drove my rental car from the Pittsburgh airport toward a long tunnel in a small mountain. The skyline of downtown Pittsburgh exploded majestically into view at the far end of that tunnel, gleaming glass towers bordered by the broad and lovely Monongahela River. Then and in my three subsequent trips to visit Fred over the years, I was always thrilled by that moment at the end of the Fort Pitt Tunnel, and by my first glimpse of the gothic, towering Cathedral of Learning on the campus of the University of Pittsburgh, both of which made me feel that I had passed into some kind of magic kingdom where there lived a godly friend.

Of course, Fred and I were not yet friends on that first trip. Intrigued by our first conversation, I had flown to Pittsburgh to interview him in person and watch a day of taping on the Neighborhood set for a longer newspaper profile on Mister Rogers himself. So I passed down from the tunnel and into the city that day, following directions to WQED television, the public station located just down the road from Pitt.

Fred himself greeted me, hurrying in my direction from the end of a long corridor. I was surprised to see him wearing glasses, because he never did on television. (He disliked fiddling with the contact lenses during taping, he told me once.) He was dressed in a white shirt and bow tie. His gray hair was neatly combed. He looked older and frailer than on television. I still remember the feel of his long, slim fingers when we shook hands for the first time. Fred grinned with delight.

"Welcome to our Neighborhood," he said.

Walking quickly (as he generally did), he led me back down the hall to the small cluster of offices of Family Communications, Inc., the nonprofit foundation he had created in 1971 to produce Mister Rogers' Neighborhood and a variety of other programs for children and families. Easily missed in the cluttered space were three gold statues, Daytime Emmy Awards that were stacked haphazardly atop a filing cabinet like neglected bookends.

"I don't know how to talk of it," Fred said when I asked him about the awards. "If it's the outside stuff that's going to nourish you . . ."

Just outside his own office were two plaster casts, relics from Fred's recent ankle injury. Now used as umbrella holders, he said he left them there as reminders of human frailty, particularly his own. He beckoned me into his corner office, a closet-sized space with rust carpet and old furniture of the sort typically found at garage sales. A crayon portrait drawn by a young boy in Oklahoma was taped to his office door. On the walls were other children's drawings sent to him from around the nation, and a handful of inspirational sayings, including this from one of his favorite books, *The Little Prince*, by Antoine de Saint-Exupery: L'essential est invisible pour les yeux. ("What is essential is invisible to the eyes.")

Fred sat on a sofa beneath a window and beckoned me to a nearby chair. I placed my running tape recorder down in front of him for an interview unlike any I had conducted before. He spoke that day of a recent episode of his program, when a young puppet in the Neighborhood of Make-Believe ran away from home, fearing that a loud argument between his parents was the harbinger of divorce. Mister Rogers then came on screen to assure his young viewers that even in loving families there could be angry times, which were not necessarily anything to worry about. Yet several of his programs in the previous few years had focused on the trauma experienced by children when the parents actually did separate. Wasn't it amazing how times had changed? Fred asked that day. (Ironically, my own marital crisis would come two years later.)

"Twenty-five years ago, if someone would have told me that in the 1990s, we would have done a whole week on divorce, I wouldn't have believed it," he said.

Which led in turn to another series of programs on anger, he said, and a Mister Rogers' song whose lyrics posed this question:

What do you do with the mad you feel when you feel so mad you could bite?

The answer, Mister Rogers would suggest to his young viewers, was pounding on clay, knocking down building blocks, kneading bread dough, and, most important, talking about difficult feelings.

"I've told [the children] there are many things you can do with your feelings that don't hurt yourself or anybody else," Fred told me in his office that day, "particularly the so-called 'negative feelings,' anger, sadness, and rage. If there's one service I feel television could offer in this world, it would be to give as many examples [as possible] of people expressing their anger in healthy ways. We see just the opposite on television."

Anger, as it turned out, was much on Fred's mind that day, and in his own heart. Five weeks before my visit, one of his oldest and closest friends, a mechanical engineer named Jim Stumbaugh, had died of cancer at his home in South Carolina. Ever since, Fred said, whenever he sat at his beloved piano, he pounded extra hard on the keys.

His childhood had not been an easy one. Until a sister was adopted when he was eleven, Fred had been the only child of loving and wealthy but overprotective parents in the small city of Latrobe, about an hour's drive from Pittsburgh. The boy was pudgy, bookish, musical, and extremely shy. Decades later, he would write of the day in grade school when a group of bullies stalked and taunted him as he walked home.

"As I walked faster, I looked around, and they started to call my name and came closer and closer and got louder and louder," Fred wrote in a book published after his death, *Life's Journeys According to Mister Rogers*. 'Freddy, hey, fat Freddy. We're going to get you, Freddy.' I resented those kids for not seeing beyond my fatness or my shyness. And I didn't know that it was all right to resent it, to feel bad about it, even to feel very sad about it. I didn't know it was all right to feel any of those things, because the advice I got from grown-ups was, 'Just let on you don't care, then nobody will bother you.'

"What I actually did was mourn. I cried to myself whenever I was alone. I cried through my fingers as I made up songs on the piano. I sought out stories of other people who were poor in spirit, and I felt for them.

"I started to look behind the things that people did and said: and little by little, concluded that Saint-Exupery was absolutely right when he wrote in *The Little Prince*: What is essential is invisible to the eyes. So after a lot of sadness, I began a lifelong search for what is essential, what it is about my neighbor that doesn't meet the eye."

Fred also would write later about the time as a teenager when he saved $19 and sent away for a Charles Atlas exercise course, hoping he could shed his doughy physique and take on the muscles of the 1940s strongman. For Fred, the Atlas course never worked, but in time that didn't matter: Fred's idea of heroes changed instead. They became people like Gandhi, Albert Schweitzer, and Jim Stumbaugh.

Stumbaugh had been Fred's classmate at Latrobe High, a star athlete, honor student, and president of his class. He and Fred had grown up attending the same church, but did not become close friends until their freshman year, when Stumbaugh suffered a kidney injury playing football and Fred volunteered to bring his schoolbooks to the hospital.

"Little did I know that that would be the beginning of a lifelong friendship," Fred said in June 1996 in his commencement address at Latrobe High, the fiftieth anniversary of his own graduation from the school. "There he was, probably the best-known, smartest, most active person in our class, and he welcomed me day after day. And what's more, he seemed to want to get to know me. I learned to trust him and told him about some of my deepest feelings, and he told me about his dad dying two years before and what that was like for him and his mom. By the time he got out of the hospital and back to school, he was telling all of his friends that that Rogers kid is OK. In fact, he quietly included me in everything he thought I'd like."

Fred always considered it a life-altering relationship, a "liberating friendship." By the time he was a senior, he was president of the student council and editor of the yearbook, "largely because I had somebody who believed in me and wasn't afraid to say so."

Fred went on to be the best man at Stumbaugh's wedding. Years after that, he was there to console Stumbaugh and his wife, Dianne, when their teenage son was killed in a traffic accident. Then, in the fall of 1995, with Stumbaugh in the final stages of a long fight against cancer, Fred flew to South Carolina to say good-bye.

In his office that day, I strained to hear as Fred's voice grew even softer than usual. He looked out the window into the brilliant autumn sun.

"Jim said to me, 'I've asked my daughter and son. I've asked my wife and now I need to ask you,'" Fred recalled. "'Is it all right to let go?'"

Fred paused as we sat together that day in his office.

"I said, 'I'm with you.' I wasn't about to ... I saw how enormous the pain was . . . He was so alive and so interested in people. He always had a dictionary nearby. He was in love with life and with learning. You hate to lose such a spirit."

So Jim Stumbaugh passed on, and Fred pounded on the keys of his piano, struggling with a nagging anger at himself that he said he could not articulate. He also felt anger toward cancer.

"With grief there is, inevitably, some times of anger and you know, God can take our anger," Fred said. "I think God respects the fact that we would share a whole gamut of feelings. I'm a real person, I think kids understand that."

It was in that next moment, I've always believed, that our friendship was born. I had become mesmerized as I sat in his office, listening to him as he remembered his friend, listening as Fred shared so much of his own insides. My mind also raced ahead, anticipating, as journalists too often do, what a wonderful story this would end up making for my newspaper. For despite the intimacy of that moment in his office, I was still a reporter and Fred was still a source. The tape recorder still lay between us, running, as if to provide a necessary barrier, enforcing the journalistic ground rules. But with Fred, there were no ground rules. There were just two people, two human beings, together. He turned away from the window, looked at me, and smiled sadly.

"You're ministering to me, Tim," he said. "By listening you minister to me."

By nine the next morning, a small army of television people had marshaled themselves around the set of Mister Rogers' Neighborhood, prepared for six hours of taping for two new episodes. I wandered about the set, admiring the famous Neighborhood Trolley on its tracks, which was the link between Mister Rogers' living room and the Neighborhood of Make-Believe. I also mingled with the crew as they waited for Fred to emerge from makeup. They were a mostly young, often vulgar and irreverent group, at least when Mister Rogers was out of earshot. One guy in particular caught my eye. Nick Tallo was the floor manager, a short, stocky man and mostly bald beneath his headset. A gold ring dangled from one ear, and tattoos crawled up both arms. By appearances alone, Fred would be more likely to keep company with a professional wrestler.

Not that Mister Rogers' Neighborhood was his only gig, Tallo told me. He worked on commercials, other television programs, and did feature films, and had in fact just finished a movie with Bill Murray. It was on that recent set, he said, that he came across a young production assistant who was incredulous when learning that Tallo's resume included twenty-nine years with Mister Rogers.

"Oh man," the younger person said. "You work for Mister Rogers! I grew up with that show! Can I come visit the set sometime? I want to thank Mister Rogers. I want to thank you."

As he waited for Fred that morning, Tallo laughed at the idea that working on a children's show would be the envy of his film industry colleagues.

"There, the bottom line is always about money," he told me. "Here, the bottom line is about kids. That's nice."

And not just children who watched Mister Rogers on television. When the star finally appeared on the set that morning, he went directly to Justin Carlson, a blond-haired, severely disabled, ten-year-old boy who sat in a wheelchair, waiting with his parents off to the side. A few months before, when the Make-A-Wish Foundation had inquired about Justin's greatest fantasy, the boy suffering from a chromosomal disorder responded with the request to meet his favorite television friend.

Justin beamed as Fred knelt by him, whispering to him from a few inches away. Then Fred helped lift him into a red wagon, a prop for that day's taping, and pulled Justin around the set, finally inviting him and his parents to sit and visit on the sofa of Mister Rogers' make-believe home. It was not a perfunctory visit. Five minutes became ten. Ten became twenty. Though Fred seemed oblivious, producer Margy Whitmer paced nearby, looking at her watch every few seconds, mumbling under her breath, "Come on, Fred. We have to get going. Please. Fred."

After a half hour she could wait no longer. Her face filled with apology, Whitmer approached the sofa where her boss sat with the Carlsons.

"I really hate to interrupt, but. . ."

David Carlson lifted his son from the sofa. Linda Carlson rose, hugged Fred, and began to weep. Like so many who watched him, the parents had wondered if the real-life Mister Rogers could ever approximate the saintly person he appeared to be on television. In a half hour in the Neighborhood, as the crew waited, they had their answer.

"Thank you very, very much," the mother said as Fred patted her shoulder. "We love you. You've helped us more than you'll ever know."

"You're so welcome, my dear," Fred said. "And I thank you for your visit."

Fred watched the family leave the set, then turned and walked briskly to the closet of his make-believe living room, where a row of his famous cardigan sweaters was neatly hung. Giving the sweaters one last look, he disappeared offstage and someone yelled for quiet.

I watched from behind the cameras as Johnny Costa, a renowned jazz pianist and the Neighborhoods longtime music director, began to play the show's theme and Fred burst through the living room door, though not in the usual Mister Rogers' fashion. This time he was wearing stylish sunglasses, a sight that caused the crew to bellow with laughter in the control room. But there was a message behind the stunt. With Fred, there was always a message.

"Do you know who I am?" Mister Rogers asked from behind his sunglasses when he had finished putting on his sweater and sneakers and the music had died down.

He pulled off the sunglasses and smiled broadly: still the same Mister Rogers. Then he put on a garish dark wig, drawing more snickers from the crew, and pulled it off, too: still Mister Rogers. No matter what he might wear on the outside, he was still Mister Rogers on the inside. The same was true of parents, Fred told his young viewers.

At the end of the first take, the crew gathered around Fred, who sat near a monitor, his boat shoes propped on a chair as he reviewed the tape.

"I think we can go on," he said, and Margy Whitmer sighed with relief.

Other Neighborhood guests arrived in succession. A woman named Marilyn gave Mister Rogers tips on how to exercise with a ball. Mr. McFeely, the Speedy Delivery man, dropped off a parcel. Another regular, Mayor Maggie, arrived with a book on sign language and demonstrated the signs for the words hello, splendid, book, fish, house and love. The sign for friend, Maggie showed Mister Rogers on the set that day, was interlocking index fingers, which seemed to fill the television host with particular delight.

Between each take, Fred sought me out to say hello and at lunch invited me onto the set for photographs. Several shots were taken of the two of us together, arms around each other's shoulders, Fred in his red sweater, the living room of Mister Rogers' home in the background. In another shot, Mr. McFeely and Mayor Maggie joined Fred and me. For a reason that I don't recall, just as the shot was taken, Fred had turned to look up at me, his face filled with a broad, affectionate, almost giddy grin.

By mid-afternoon the shooting was almost done. In the last scene of the day, Mister Rogers would explain to his young audience how his television set was constructed. When he had finished, the crew once more gathered around their boss, who propped up his feet, sipping fruit juice through a straw as he reviewed the video.

"I'd like to try again," he said.

Some in the crew stifled moans.

"Oh," said Margy Whitmer, the surprised producer. "OK. What would you like to do differently?"

"A few things," Fred replied without specifying, and he strode back to the set.

In the next take, he changed only a few words, but in his mind, his meaning was clearer.

"Thank you for indulging me," he said when he had again reviewed the tape. "I think that segment was much nicer."

Then Fred rose from his chair, sat down at Costa's piano, and began to play a tune from the 1940s. It was a Neighborhood ritual that said work for the day was finally done.

I met Fred at WQED the next morning, a Saturday, for one more visit and to say good-bye. The older of Fred's two sons, Jay, and his two young grandsons had come to visit that morning, too, so Fred took the boys down to the set and allowed them to play there for several minutes. When Jay and his sons had gone, Fred and I sat down together in his office. He called his wife at home.

"My dear, I wanted you to meet the young man I was telling you about last night," Fred said to Joanne Rogers, then handed the phone to me.

As Joanne and I chatted, Fred pulled out his camera and took my picture, grinning. Later, Fred quizzed me about my family, my job, and my favorite things. When I described my love of the mountains, he told me about his love of the sea. When our conversation turned to books, he told me that his favorite writer was a Catholic priest named Henri Nouwen. Had I heard of him? Until that moment, I had not, but told Fred that I was determined to find Nouwen's books as soon as I returned to Texas.

Fred hugged me at the front door of the television station when we finally said goodbye, telling me I was welcome in his Neighborhood anytime. By then it was mid-afternoon, another brilliant autumn day in a beautiful, bustling section of Pittsburgh. I walked slowly toward my nearby hotel through the sunshine, feeling almost disoriented by what I had experienced the previous three days. Throughout my life, I had been blessed by the love and friendship of many extraordinary people, but somehow, this man was different, a person possessed of an otherworldly purity and goodness. My newspaper assignment had thus become a pilgrimage, of sorts, a once-in-a-lifetime opportunity, or so I assumed, to experience that sort of historic kindness. I knew it was a time I would always remember.

Not scheduled to fly back to Texas until the next afternoon, I decided to celebrate my good fortune with a pizza in my hotel room, and watch a college football game between the University of Texas and Texas A&M. The pizza had just been delivered and it was seconds away from kickoff when the telephone rang in my room. I expected it to be my wife, calling from Texas to say hello. But when I answered, I again heard that voice.

"Tim, this is Fred Rogers," he said, as if I wouldn't have otherwise known. "If you don't have other plans, I was wondering whether you'd like to join my family and me for church tomorrow."

I'm sure I stammered in my reply.

On a rainy Sunday morning, I followed Fred's directions to Sixth Presbyterian Church, an old stone sanctuary in the affluent Squirrel Hill neighborhood of Pittsburgh. Fred waited for me in the vestibule with his two grandsons, introduced me to his pastor and several of his friends in the congregation, then finally tracked down his wife, a short, vivacious woman with a jolly laugh. Joanne Rogers, dressed in a choir robe, greeted me warmly before hurrying away to prepare for the service.

Though an ordained Presbyterian minister himself, Fred's pastoral work was considered to be his television program, so at church he was just another member of the congregation and a regular at Sunday morning Bible study classes. That morning, Fred, his two grandsons, and I found a pew near the front of the sanctuary. I remember consciously trying to freeze each surreal moment as I stood next to Fred and sang hymns, and watched him wrestle with his fidgety grandchildren in the pew. I can attest that even Mister Rogers became exasperated with little kids in church.

It was midway through the service when the pastor asked if anyone wished to publicly share their joys or concerns. Several in the congregation rose to speak of a relative or friends suffering in some way. Others stood to give thanks for a successful surgery, or a new baby, or a promotion at work. The old woman behind us at the back of the church spoke last. She began with a vague complaint about the Gulf War, then took up against Vietnam, and the president, and members of Congress and generals, and anyone else who, in her mind, might have had something to do with the death of American soldiers. The diatribe went on for at least five minutes. People throughout the church began to squirm in the pews. At the pulpit, the pastor shifted from foot to foot and stared down at his notes in embarrassment. I stifled an impulse to turn and look back at the woman, who, as the minutes passed, began to seem deranged. When her long rant finally ended, there was an audible sigh of relief in the church. Most in the congregation were clearly mortified, but not the man sitting next to me. The moment the old woman finished and the service resumed, Fred leaned over and whispered in my ear.

"The poor dear," he said. "You can be sure that at some time in her past, she suffered a great personal loss because of war."

After the service, Fred hurried from his pew, found the old woman, where she stood alone in the back of the church, said a few tender words, and gave her a hug.

After the service, Fred and a grandson walked me several blocks through the misty morning to where my rental car was parked. He hugged me again.

"I'm very glad you and I are friends," he said.

I watched Fred and the boy start back toward the church through the rain. A half-block away, he stopped, turned back toward me, and smiled broadly, raising his interlocked index fingers, recalling Mayor Maggie's sign language lesson from two days before: friendship. That night, when I had arrived home in Texas, my wife said there was something I needed to hear on our telephone answering machine. Once again, it was that voice.

"Catherine," the voice said. "This is Fred Rogers, calling from Pittsburgh. I just wanted to thank you for sharing your husband with all of us here in my Neighborhood."

Chapter 3

My profile of Mister Rogers, which included a passage describing Fred's grief over the death of Jim Stumbaugh, was published in the *Star-Telegram* on Christmas Eve 1995, and later was picked up by several other newspapers across the country. "Thanks so much for your obvious care in writing that so beautifully," Fred wrote in a January postcard from Winter Park, Florida, where he and his wife vacationed every winter. "I've just finished ten new scripts (my assignment from Margy!) so you know the relief." A few weeks later, he sent me a letter he had received from the mother of another disabled boy who had visited the set of Mister Rogers' Neighborhood about a year before the boy died.

"The other day I saw a long article in our local paper," the mother wrote to Fred. "I kept it and reread it. . . and today I want to take the opportunity to express my deepest sympathy in the loss of your best friend, Jim Stumbaugh. As he influenced your life in such a significant way, I am convinced he lives on in you and your ways of influencing so many lives in so many ways."

The mother had obviously referred to my story, Fred said in an accompanying note, because I was the only reporter he had talked with about the death of Jim. "I thought you might like to see how your words touched her," he said. "Know that I think of you often and wish you every blessing. [I'm] grateful for your friendship."

I couldn't help but wonder: Why would this celebrity, however kindly he might be, choose to invest in a relationship with a person like me? Yet gradually, in the weeks and months after we met in Pittsburgh, my remaining skepticism dissolved and I came to believe that he was wholly genuine when he described his pleasure in our new relationship. ("Yes, please do keep in touch," he wrote two months after we met. "I'm delighted that you would want to.") I had worried that he would consider me a nuisance because I wrote to him so often, every few weeks at least, also sending along recent newspaper stories of mine that I thought might interest him (or that he might be impressed by). But each time I did, a thoughtful and heartfelt reply showed up in my mailbox within days, as if Fred had nothing better to do than promptly answer my mail.

Among the stories I sent to him was one that described my four-day stay at Kent's Nursing Home in Fort Worth, where I had watched some old people die, others plow on through their infirmity and loneliness, and where I was befriended by a wonderful man named Hal Thomas, a nursing home resident in his mid-nineties.

"Any wonder you're proud of the Kent piece!" Fred wrote. "It's masterfully composed. You obviously know how to introduce your readers to the complexities of life in ways which pull us right along with the story. I felt I knew Hal . . . and the others you describe so well. What a superb article! Thanks for your gracious thoughtful note and self."

Fred's remarkable compassion, it turned out, extended to another of my subjects, a paroled child molester who was, in Fred's words, "doing his best to live with his compulsions."

"You write so well, always showing at least two sides to the issue," Fred wrote after reading that story. "As (his mentor, the theologian William Orr) said, The only thing evil can't stand is forgiveness.' Imagine evil disappearing in the atmosphere of forgiveness!"

Then, in mid May of 1996, I sent along my tribute to Hal Thomas, my friend from the nursing home, who had died a few days earlier. The essay began by describing Hal's morning ritual: bacon and eggs, greeting the nursing home cat, and studying the newspaper obituaries, his nose a few inches from the copy as he peered intently through a large magnifying glass. Once satisfied, Hal would lean back in his wheelchair and say with great satisfaction, "I'm not in there." Alas, on May 13, 1996, my friend was finally "in there," and I missed him greatly.

I had met Hal during a nursing home bingo game, "an inopportune moment to make his acquaintance," I wrote, "for he focused on the bingo cards arrayed before him with the intensity of a laser." He was a large man, built like a panda, with a big head, wisps of white hair that he kept meticulously combed, thick glasses, and jowls of loose skin about the throat. Hal had worked at the telephone company for many years and kept a small farm where he grew eighty-pound watermelons, until a fall had forced him into the nursing home. Female residents there, generally younger women in their seventies and eighties, quarreled over who would sit at his table for lunch, or hold his hand during nursing home activities. It didn't help that Hal was an inveterate flirt.

'They're all my girlfriends," he'd boast. But he still grieved for his wife, who had died six years earlier, and for his mother, who had passed when Hal was a child. All of his siblings were dead, too, as was one of his four children. Constant grief was a fact of life when you were his age, as I learned on a walk with Hal on the evening we met.

It was a lovely late-summer night, warm but not hot. The fading sun turned the brick of Trimble Tech High School just down the street a brilliant orange. Hal refused assistance as he pulled himself up from his wheelchair, clutching the pole of a No Parking sign for support. Then, using his chair for a walker, he shuffled up a slight incline toward the high school.

In a few minutes, he returned to his wheelchair, leading us back to a large live oak where we stopped to enjoy the night. Hal spoke of his farm, and the night he fell, crawling halfway across his house to call for help.

"The following day, my son said, 'Dad, I talked to Dr. Davidson, and he said you'll never walk again,'" Hal said as I knelt next to his wheelchair. "I said, 'I will walk.' And I did."

Hal said living in a nursing home depressed him at first, but he felt better now.

"What made you feel better?" I asked.

"John, three-sixteen," he said.

I didn't understand.

"John, three-sixteen," he repeated.

Then I remembered the ubiquitous placard held up at sporting events. John 3-16.

"I think I know that one," I said. "Who shall ever believeth in Me shall never die."

"You forgot the first part," Hal said. "God so loved the world..."

He couldn't finish the sentence. His lips quivered and the sounds of his quiet sobs mixed with the birdsong. I touched his arm and waited out his sorrow.

"Excuse me," Hal said finally. "I was thinking about my brothers and sisters."

In a few minutes the emotion passed and we resumed our talk. Hal told me of new purposes in life, like watching the nursing home's front door so fellow residents didn't wander off unnoticed, or staying active in the telephone company credit union or reading the Bible.

"What makes you happiest in life?" I asked him.

He paused to carefully consider the question.

"Bingo, I guess," he replied.

Periodically, over my four days at Kent's, I left Hal to meet other residents. Ethel Kingsley, Kent's oldest resident at age 105, remembered Indiana grain harvests from the 1890s. My roommate, Lovis Robinson, was a blind man in his eighties who listened to gospel music all night and occasionally confused me with his wife. The woman named Julia, who reminded me of Lauren Bacall without teeth, wandered into my room one day and made off with a pair of my slacks, which an aide later found, neatly folded near Julia's bed.

But I always returned to Hal's room. In the morning, he read the obits while I pored over the box scores. He told me Aggie jokes over coffee, and conveniently dozed off when I was beating him at checkers.

My third day at the nursing home, I rode in the backseat as Hal sat sullenly in the car of his son, Ben, a seventy-year-old retired dentist. We were headed to Hal's farm, his first trip back since his fall, and by his demeanor it was clear that Hal would have just as soon let the past alone.

But at the farm, Hal found things almost as he had left them. Horses grazed in the pasture. Chickens cackled in the meadow. Water still flowed from an old well. Hal made his way inside the large white farmhouse, pushing a walker.

"Fond memories," Hal said.

At the end of the half-hour visit, the property's new owner, Alexandra Orozco, followed Hal to his son's car. She began to weep as she leaned to hug him in the passenger seat.

"You have nothing to worry about, Mr. Thomas," she said. "You come back any time. I just wanted you to know that your place is being taken good care of."

"OK," Hal said.

Late that night, Hal sat outside in the nursing home courtyard in his cap and plaid pajamas, replaying the day.

"That old well is still there," he said. "I drank many drops of water out of that well."

He was pleased that the new owner had pruned the rose bushes he had planted years earlier.

"The stars are bright tonight," he said.

In a few minutes, a nurse's aide came to take him inside and put him to bed. Hal handed over his dentures, his glasses. The aide leaned him back on his bed, pulled off his socks and black slippers, and elevated his swollen feet with pillows. I looked down at him and said goodnight.

Hal smiled.

"I'll see you in my dreams," he said.

I saw Hal many more times in the months after my nursing home stay. I lent him my monster mask for the nursing home Halloween party, and bought him a Texas wildflower calendar for his ninety-fourth birthday. But generally, my visits were brief moments stolen from a busy life.

When I did stop by to see him, I began to notice that Hal was changing. His mouth and shoulders sagged. He seemed despondent and I worked harder and harder to coax out a grin or an Aggie joke. Hal was tired. He was ready to see his parents, siblings, and deceased daughter again. I knew I was watching a friend die.

Someday soon, I told myself week after week, I would make time to sit with him, talk to him, find out what was on his mind as the end neared, play one last game of checkers. Next week, I said. Next week.

The last time I saw Hal was during one of those hurried visits to the nursing home. He was sitting near the front door, awake but groggy. I shook Hal's hand and promised to return when I had more time. Next week.

But when friends are ninety-four, sometimes there are no next weeks. Not long after I saw him, Hal's liver failed, and he died in his room on a Saturday night.

I write this more than a week after his death, an exercise in remembering. God knows Hal deserved rest, relief from his suffering, reunion with his family, but I have been deprived of a friend who shared with me the wisdom and goodness of his ninety-four years.

I am sad and irritable. Hal is constantly in my thoughts, I will miss him always.

When I sent Fred that essay, I told him in a note how much I had grown to love the old man, how much Hal's love for me had enriched my life in such a short time, how, because of the death of Hal, I had a greater appreciation for the grief Fred felt over the loss of Jim Stumbaugh. Fred's reply arrived less than a week later.

"Your letter and your article about Hal Thomas really touched me," Fred wrote. "You are such a gifted man (as I've told you) not only by your writing, but by your investment of yourself in friendship. You say that Mr. Thomas enriched your life. I can only begin to imagine how your delight in his life enriched him."

Thus went our early correspondence—my letters and stories sent to Fred (we had yet to begin communicating via e-mail, and I would not presume to bother him on the telephone, at least not then), and his warm, wise, complimentary, and encouraging words I received in return. Because of the pitch-perfect love of his letters, it sometimes seemed then, as it did throughout our friendship, that I was corresponding with God himself. Gradually, the specter of Mister Rogers, the television celebrity, figured less and less in my thoughts about him. Instead, he was Fred, a celestial font of affirmation, a wise and loving older man who seemed determined to shower me with the sort of unconditional regard I had always craved, and just at the time in my life when I needed it most.

My son Patrick was six years old that hot spring morning, a rather chunky boy with brown hair, and cheeks full of freckles, who desperately wanted to please his father. So after winning his first race on his first field day, he rushed up to me beaming, blue ribbon in hand. But that event had been a straight-ahead sprint, and the next, an obstacle course, was sure to be more difficult. Sure enough, early in the race, Patrick tripped and fell heavily, sprawled in the dirt in front of all of his classmates. He rose and began to run, but tripped again at the next obstacle and fell. I watched helplessly as tears of humiliation began to pour down his cheeks. Somehow, Patrick found the courage to get to his feet and stumble across the finish line long after all of the other kids. He was sobbing by the time I could get to him and take him into my arms.

At home later that night, I shut off his cartoons to tell Patrick that I was more proud of him for getting up and finishing that difficult second race than for winning the first one, and judging by his broad smile, he seemed to understand. It was a moment as a father that I will always remember. (My Christmas present from my son that year was the fifth-place ribbon he had been awarded for finishing that difficult race.)

But as I tried to console Patrick, I could not help seeing myself in the dirt at his age. It seems that I spent a lot of time there as a boy, both literally and figuratively, feeling different from other boys because of my sensitivity and bookishness, afraid and humiliated by my weakness. But instead of a father who would gather me into his arms to reassure me, what I remembered was his silence and an ashamed look on his face that for years made my heart sink whenever I thought of it.

That wound and what I've come to understand as a chronic depression that had afflicted our family for generations was at the core of the despair that threatened to consume me in the mid-1990s. My journals from that time describe the life of a man who was preoccupied with and nearly overwhelmed by his own suffering. Ironically, it was also a time when one journalism award followed another. In 1996 and 1997 I was named the Star Reporter of Texas by a leading journalism foundation in Austin, the first time one reporter had received the state's most prestigious journalism honor in consecutive years. There were other state and national awards, and my stories were regularly being published in national magazines and book anthologies. But the success and recognition that I had pursued for decades, which I had sought as an antidote for my shame and insecurity, did nothing to alleviate my inner torment and, if anything, made it worse. I felt like a fraud. No matter how much recognition came my way, I felt like a weak kid in the dirt.

"I can't continue to live this way," I wrote one day in a typical journal entry from that time. "I feel so full of shame and depression, anger. My life is slipping away. The beauty of it goes by me unnoticed because I'm so wrapped up in myself.

"I was thinking recently about the first moment my father's sperm and my mother's egg united, what a miracle that was and how every moment of my life has flowed from there. But that miracle was not meant to be lived this way. Waking up every morning, there is depression and fear about what the day will bring. I just am not up to the task of life. I feel that I am fundamentally defective."

Another day during the depths of the Furies, shortly after being named the Star Reporter of Texas, I again poured out my despair into my journal.

"I don't want to be here anymore," I wrote that day. "Life seems so gray. Don't know what to do. Want to go back to sleep and sleep the rest of the day. Hide from the world."

But instead of hiding from the world, I wrote newspaper stories, prayed every day for relief, talked to a therapist, and took my medicine. Eventually, I also did something else. Whether it was an act of inspiration, desperation, or a combination of the two, I will never be sure. But I decided to write to my friend in Pittsburgh and tell him the difficult truth of my life.

My letter, dated June 22, 1996, began by thanking Fred for his friendship, and telling him of my plans for the summer. Those plans, I said, included writing a story about the religious faith of Johnny Oates, the manager of the Texas Rangers baseball team, a trip to Minnesota for my twentieth high school reunion, a long weekend in New York with my wife, and a solo camping excursion to Colorado sometime in August.

The purpose of this letter, however, is not to bring you up-to-date on the details of my life, though I'm very glad to do so. The purpose, Fred, is that I have something to ask of you.

The last several years have been a very profound time of intense personal pain and great healing, a time of great self-discovery as I've tried to come to terms with the realities of my life, past and present. At the forefront of my mind and soul right now is how hard I tried to get my dad to be proud of me, through sports, through school, through the way I tried to be obedient and good. But no matter what I did, it never seemed enough. I could never wrest from him the love and sense of acceptance that I so desperately craved as a child, and have been craving ever since.

I realize now that God is the ultimate source for that kind of love and acceptance. But I also have realized that I have gravitated toward older men in my life, without really knowing why. Now I think I know. Hal Thomas, for one, was an older man who loved me without restraint or without condition. In short, I think Hal was proud of me, not for what I did, but for the person I was, because I was enough of a person to have a capacity for friendship.

Hal was proud of me. How terribly important to me I now realize that is. I read Henri Nouwen this morning, and several chapters in [the book of]

Matthew, and meditated for a long time on my pain, and realized what I need to do. It is this. There are several men older than me who have become very important in my life. And one by one I plan to ask them this. "Will you be proud of me?"

That is the question I have of you this morning, Fred. Will you be proud of me? It would mean a great deal to me if you would. I have come to love you in a very special way. In your letters, and during our brief time together in Pittsburgh, you have done so much to teach me how to be a person and a man. And now I have this favor to ask of you.

Will you be proud of me?

As I sit this morning, I grapple with great inner pain, but I also feel the gentle guiding hand of God in mine. My life has taken on a depth, and a beauty that years ago I never would have believed possible.

I hope this letter finds you, your family and friends well and happy.

With much love and gratitude,

Tim

I cringe when reading those words now, marveling that a man soon to be forty years old could be so childlike and vulnerable, particularly with another man. I've shared my insides with many other trusted mentors over the years, but never with such a lack of restraint. Despite what I told Fred in that letter, it was the only time I would openly make that request of another man. That I did so with Fred was a measure of my intuitive faith in his goodness, and I fully expected a kind and compassionate reply. What I did not expect was the letter from Fred that, as much as any therapy or medication, set me on the road to true healing.

July 1, 1996

Dear Tim,

The answer to your question is

"YES"

a resounding YES . . .

I will be proud of you. I am proud of you. I have been proud of you since first we met. I'm deeply touched that you would offer so much of yourself to me, and look forward to knowing all that you would care to share in the future. Nothing you could tell me could change my YES for you. Please remember that.

You are the only person who has come for an interview who came to church with me. I wonder if you realize how special you really are!? Your place in this life is unique—absolutely unique. I feel blessed to be one of your friends. Only God can arrange such mutually trusting relationships—-for sure! For sure!!

YES, Tim, YES.

Love, Fred

From that time until his death seven years later, in almost every one of the scores of letters and e-mail messages he sent, my friend signed off with IPOY (I'm Proud of You) an acronym that is forever stamped on my heart.

But what has come to be known in my family as the "IPOY letter" was only the beginning of one of the most intensely difficult yet therapeutic periods of my life, a couple of years when I poured out my rawest feelings in letters to Pittsburgh, and received Fred's healing words in return.

July 22, 1996

Dear Fred,

. . . Generations of my family will see [the IPOY letter] and treasure it as such an extraordinary expression of love and acceptance

. . . There are the makings of compassion in my heart, but on balance, I'm still consumed with my own pain, praying that God will take it away I'm ready to keep walking through it until He does. He has never failed me before.

Writing this has helped me be aware of the blessings of my life—too numerous to mention—and your friendship is so very high on that list, with my children . . . a marriage to a remarkable woman that to me grows more and more sacred by the day ... (I hope you and Catherine can meet each other someday. You would both be enriched by that.) . . . Dear friends and family who have always loved and supported me. . . Hal Thomas. . . trees and mountains and oceans. . . baseball. . . books. . . Henri Nouwen . . . and on and on.

I read recently in one of Henri's writings that Christ didn't come to take away our sufferings, but to share in them. I love that little "footsteps" story in which the man on the beach who feels deserted by God during life's most difficult times is actually being carried by God during them.

I am being carried! There is no greater proof than your friendship.

Much love,

Tim

July 26, 1996

Dear Tim,

. . . Your expression of gratitude in this life is so touching. Amid your pain, you're still able to see trees and mountains and oceans and baseball and books and friends and Catherine and God's redemptive hand in all that you do and are. To say that you are being carried is a declaration of enormous faith and hope.

Please know how grateful I am for you, Tim. Real friendships work both ways. Your trust confirms my trustworthiness, your love, my loving. I am proud of you and honored to be your friend. . .

Love and peace,
Fred

Aug. 19, 1996
My dear Tim,
Your wonderful "letter from High Camp" allowed me to feel that I was right beside you. You write with such beauty and such feeling. I'm so grateful that you allow me to be a guest in your inner life. Your trust enriches me beyond any words that I have.

Your patience in allowing God to remove the "roadblock" will serve you all your days. That you could go within yourself and contemplate God's love for you is a gift without measure. You and God can rejoice together about such grace!!

Love,
Fred
Again, my thanks for your wonderful letter. IPOY
F.

Oct. 2, 1996
Dear, dear Tim,
Not only you, but your letter itself is a masterpiece—truly!! I don't know when I've read a more beautiful letter filled with sadness and hope and understanding and truth and (as I said to you on the phone) TRUST. As I read it I had such an urge to hug you. You are such a wonderfully deep human being, Tim, and those of us who love you and are loved by you are a truly blessed band.

You can be assured of my prayers "for that continued healing." As always I ask for yours. And count me in as we celebrate the truth (of which you speak—write—so eloquently), and the freedom that truth brings.

To be sure, IPOY. There's no way anyone can make you believe it. All I can do is say it from the deepest place of my being.

Fred

June 30, 1998

Dear Tim,

You're an amazing man, my friend. I'm so glad to hear from you. Your telling of Patrick's first grade field day had me practically in tears. I say you're amazing because without the kind of support you obviously needed from your dad (the kind we all need from our dads) I wonder how in the world you're able to give that to Patrick. But obviously you do. You've turned out to be a man not of contempt, but one filled with compassion, with the ability to give "consolation." Patrick's so blessed to have you as a father.

Today we were taping "interiors" and getting a good deal done when all of the sudden lightning struck and all the lights, cameras, everything electric in the building went OUT. We thought it would be a temporary thing; but as the afternoon wore on, we realized that we wouldn't be able to finish our day's work. I don't think that has ever happened to me before in the studio. There were a lot of damaged trees all over the streets. It took me an hour and fifteen minutes to get home from work, a trip that takes seven minutes at most!!

We'll have to make up what we couldn't tape on Friday and next Tuesday. I welcome your prayers. My daily swim serves me well for being as calm as possible during those times. In fact, as I was driving home, running into one street after another that had been blocked by fallen trees, I thought, "You can choose to let this bother you or let this be an adventure and welcome the challenge. Happily, with plenty of gas in my car and some gorgeous ancient music sung by "Anonymous 4 " I inched my way home: content to be alive and well and blessed by a wonderful life.

You're an important part of that life, Tim. I'm grateful to God for you.

My love is with you always. Fred

PS. Joanne drove the station wagon to Nantucket. She'll be flying back here tomorrow. Our kids will use the house until we go in late August and stay for three weeks. P.P.S. (Most importantly} IPOY F.

September 17, 1996
Dear Tim,
Know that I am with you . . . always. Fred

Chapter 4

In July 1996, in the letter that followed his first IPOY, Fred wrote to say he was puzzled. "I'm curious to know where your enormous capacity for affection comes from," he said. "Someone loved you early or otherwise I don't see how you could be so loving now."

What's more, he said, "I don't understand the roots of your anger and pain in your relationship with your father. Maybe you'll tell me more about that."

Fred clearly wanted to know more about my dad, wondering what his childhood was like. Fred's compassion extended to my dad as well. So I started telling Fred what I knew, starting from my first memories of the godlike figure of my boyhood. My father's name is LaMoure Jerome Madigan, though for some reason everyone in my hometown knew him as "Myke": a relatively short fellow, but built like a linebacker, dark-haired and ruggedly handsome. He had been a star high school football and basketball player in the little North Dakota town where he grew up, and, when he whipped the town bully, gained a local reputation as a guy not to be messed with. My dad later came within a whisker of playing college football in Washington, was nearly killed while working construction on a giant dam, and served in the army in postwar Germany. Then he came home to marry my mom and go into the lumber business in the small town of Crookston, Minnesota. He came to be the foremost lumber expert in that place, and I was sure my dad could pound a nail faster and cut a board straighter than any other living soul.

In short, he was a man's man, a rugged character straight from John Wayne movies, at least in my boyish mind—everything that I so clearly was not. And try as he might, my dad could not mask his disappointment when I would flinch from a ground ball in baseball; or withdraw from a body check in hockey; or slink away from boyhood fistfights; or refuse to go to Boy Scout camp because I didn't want to be away from home; or quit playing football my freshman year in high school because I was too small and the game was too rough. To all those things in early boyhood, I preferred books instead.

Two memories stand out in particular. One concerned the local neighborhood ritual we called "sleeping out," which was what passed for adventure among ten-year-old boys in the town where I grew up. Every week or so during the summer, a group of us hauled our sleeping bags into a tent that was pitched in someone's backyard, spent the night, and woke up to have pillow fights the next morning. Only I rarely made it to the pillow fight. For reasons I would never understand, long after the other boys were snoring next to me, I would lie awake in the tent, struggling to sleep, praying to doze off so I could wake up the next morning with my friends. But sleep would never come. So eventually I snuck back home in my underwear, pillow beneath my arm (I can still feel the cold, dewy grass on my bare feet, and the shame), slinking back into my own bed in the basement of our house. In the parlance of the neighborhood, that was known as "chickening out." My dad never said anything about such cowardice that I can recall, but I almost wish he had. Instead, he would look at me and shake his head, or he would silently eat his breakfast cereal at the dining room table, obviously roiling inside at the notion that the oldest of his seven children (five of them boys) could be such a sissy.

The second memory was of a night in the winter of my sophomore year in high school. By the time I was a senior, I had grown to be tall and strong, and as fierce a competitor in baseball and ice hockey as my dad had ever been. But on the night in question, I remained scrawny and timid. A rival team filled with big and nasty players had humiliated our high school hockey team that night and I had spent much of the game cowering. When I got home, my dad was sitting in his chair at the far end of our living room, next to the stereo. I remember he was still wearing his heavy winter coat. And he could choke back his disgust no longer. Though I don't remember his exact words, they came gushing from his mouth at the top of his lungs, and his meaning would never be forgotten. I was weak, a sissy, and if I could not find a backbone, I would do well to find a sport other than hockey. I finally could take no more, and fled from the room in tears.

My brother Steve, who was a year younger, was willful and more rebellious, and he and my father openly locked horns over the years. I kept silent, believing down deep what my father said and felt about me in those days to be true. I continued to feel weak and ashamed for years thereafter, even after I had become a star high school athlete myself; even after I went off as an adult to camp alone in mountain wilderness (perhaps to prove to myself I wasn't a chicken after all); even after I became an award-winning author and journalist.

"Inwardly, to be honest, I write today with a great weight bearing down on my soul," I wrote to Fred later in 1996. "The anger toward my father—anger from the past—threatens to consume me at times, and makes healthy loving and living very difficult.

"My prayer is now, Fred, that the Lord will soften my heart."

Eventually, my prayers were answered, thanks largely to the support and guidance of Fred and other close friends. Inspired by their curiosity, I began to question my dad on visits home to Minnesota, wondering about his childhood, of which I knew very little until then. It was not something he often talked about, and as I began to probe, it became obvious why that was. Though he tried to minimize his own heartbreak, it was clear his boyhood home was a place of far too much alcohol and far too little love.

"I would bet that my dad's father never once told him he loved him, never once gave him a hug," I told Fred in a letter.

His boyhood also came at the height of the Great Depression, and my dad's family was greatly afflicted by the poverty of the time. My father was only sixteen when his dad died of a stroke, but because there was no money in the family for a gravedigger, he did the job himself.

The most telling moment in my quest to understand my dad came in the summer of 1996, when he and I drove alone together through the little town of Underwood, North Dakota, the place where he grew up. I asked him to show me where his house had been, where his father's cafe had stood, where he had played football and basketball. As we drove that day, I asked how often his mother and father had come to watch him play sports. I was shocked by his reply.

"Twice," my dad immediately replied, spitting out a fact that obviously had been at the center of his own battered heart for a half-century. "My mother came to watch me play basketball twice."

I immediately pictured my dad as a teenager, and all the games when he must have stolen glances toward the sidelines, looking for his own father to come and pick him up out of the proverbial dirt, all the times of bitter disappointment when my grandfather did not. My heart was broken—not for my own old hurts, but for my father and his.

"It seems that the more you can 'hear' your Dad's pain, the more understanding and less resentful you are," Fred wrote when I told him that story. "If nobody was proud of him, how could he be proud of anybody—including himself and his son!?!?"

And as I began to understand my dad, other memories of my childhood crowded back into my heart. I remembered so many Little League mornings, standing in the dewy outfield grass, watching our yellow station wagon pull up by the baseball field, and the stocky, handsome man walk over to watch the game, leaning on the fence with his elbows. His father had never seen him play, but my dad never missed one of my baseball or hockey games, not one in all my years growing up. No matter what was happening at his work, the yellow station wagon always pulled up by the field. My dad might have muttered at times about my performance, but he was always there.

I remembered how he brought home a box of peppermint hearts for each of his seven kids every Valentine's Day.

I remembered the small, wooden airplane hangar he built for us one Christmas, a gift his children promptly ignored. Yet as an adult I pictured him working alone after hours in the cold basement of the lumberyard, sawing and nailing and neatly painting that hangar, a gift from his own hands.

I remembered the twilight games of backyard catch with him when he was already exhausted from a long day at work, and my pride at making his hand burn with the speed of my fastball.

I remembered what a wonderful dancer he was, twirling my mother around the floor, doing the polka at small-town wedding receptions.

I remembered his beautiful tenor voice as he sang hymns at our Catholic church, and watching him kneel by his bed to say the rosary nearly every day during Lent.

I remembered his utter devotion to my mother, and to his own mother, who had come to live near us in a nursing home.

I remembered his artistic side, how he spent hours over the drafting board as one of the most sought-after home designers in that part of northern Minnesota.

I remembered how no businessman in our town was thought to have more integrity.

And I remembered the tortured set of his face as he came through the door at the end of the day, and the long sighs, recognizing in them someone who had suffered from the same terrible depression that probably would have killed me without therapy and medication. I knew from dreadful experience that the illness made it almost impossible to fully love, nearly impossible to be emotionally connected to the people around you, no matter how much you might care for them. In the time of my father's greatest suffering, however, antidepressants and therapy remained largely taboo, especially for men. So he was left to suffer, and I realize now that he did so nobly and courageously. That he functioned as well as he did, I consider nothing less than a miracle.

Yes, I desperately wanted him to take me into his arms when I was young and tell me that he loved me despite my weakness. But he had given me much more than he had been given as a boy, so much more. I also came to understand that he was never a god. He was just a man, a suffering man, doing the best he could. In other words, he was a man just like me.

And my dad did love me deeply. Of that, there was never any doubt. After I had gone to college and then into the newspaper world, he always hugged me at the end of my visits home, and told me he loved me when we said good-bye. Like so many other men of his era, my dad was loath to show his emotions. But after my visits home as a young adult, when my car had pulled away, I was told that he would sit alone in his rocking chair and sob for hours.

Chapter 5

In late summer of 1996, Fred wrote to say that he and I would soon have a chance to take up our deepening friendship in person.

"Tim, we're going to Chicago Oct. 12 to be with Henri (Nouwen) as he receives the Ronald McDonald Charities Award; and, we've decided to fly from there to Fort Worth the next day," Fred wrote on August 18. On the trip south, he and Joanne planned to visit one of their longtime friends, the famous classical pianist and Fort Worth resident, Van Cliburn. "Of course I want to see you and meet Catherine and have you both get to know Joanne. I have no idea what Van will cook up, but Joanne has already made a [hotel] reservation so the ball is beginning to roll. I so look forward to being with you again."

It was fitting that Nouwen should somehow figure in our reunion. He and Fred were good friends who had corresponded regularly for years. (In one of his later books, *Sabbatical Journey*, Nouwen wrote of calling to console Fred after the death of Jim Stumbaugh. "At 6:00 P.M. I called Fred in Pittsburgh to tell him about our prayers for Jim. Fred told me that he had just played on his piano all the songs he and Jim used to sing together," Nouwen wrote. "It was his way of mourning. He was truly grateful for my call. On a day like this I marvel over the gift of friendship.")

From my first trip to Pittsburgh, the Dutch priest's books had also been a regular part of my daily spiritual reading, and frequently and appreciatively mentioned in my own early correspondence with Fred. I was deeply moved by how Nouwen wrote about the relationship between spirituality and human brokenness, including his own. He was a man who had taught at Harvard and Yale, and was among the world's most widely read spiritual writers, but one who wrote transparently about his own insecurity and loneliness, and who felt most at home in the slums of Peru, or in the community of mentally handicapped people near Toronto, where he had lived since the mid 1980s.

"The authentic spiritual life finds its basis in the human condition, which all people—whether they are Christian or not—have in common," Nouwen wrote once. In another of his books, *The Wounded Healer*, Nouwen wrote that a minister's service "will not be perceived as authentic unless it comes from a heart wounded by the suffering about which he speaks . . . The great illusion of leadership is to think that others can be led out of the desert by someone who has never been there."

Nouwen, clearly, had been there, which was one of the reasons Fred and I admired his work so much. In fact, it was Fred who, in 1996, mailed me a copy of *The Inner Voice of Love: A Journey Through Anguish to Freedom*, calling it one of the priest's finest books because it was his "most personal, which is often the most universal."

"This book is my secret journal," Nouwen wrote in the Introduction. "It was written during the most difficult period of my life, from December 1987 to June 1988. That was a time of extreme anguish, during which I wondered whether I would be able to hold onto my life. Everything came crashing down— my self-esteem, my energy to live and work, my sense of being loved, my hope for healing, my trust in God. . . everything. Here I was, a writer about the spiritual life, known as someone who loves God and gives hope to people, flat on the ground and in total darkness."

Which quite nearly described my own emotional and spiritual state in the summer of 1996, Fred knew, and my friend from Pittsburgh surely appreciated how Nouwen's experience would be a source of hope and healing for me. Nouwen, I would also learn, had worked through a painful and complicated relationship with his own father. Because we had so much in common, Fred said, he hoped to introduce the two of us some day.

"I hope for this because I know Henri will be nourished by you just as you feel he has enhanced your life," Fred said.

But Nouwen and I would never meet, nor would Fred ever visit Fort Worth. In mid-September, I heard Fred on my voice mail at work and received a short letter from him a few days later.

9/ 18/96 Dear Tim,

Tried calling both your office and home today. Maybe you're out of town. I may have sounded distraught. Anyway, Henri [Nouwen] had a heart attack in Holland. He was just about to leave for Russia to make a film about [one of his recent books] and got ill. He's going to have to have complete rest for quite a while so our trip to Chicago-Fort Worth has been postponed indefinitely. Disappointed, but grateful that something can be done about Henri's health. MDs are trying medication first to dissolve blood clot in lower quadrant.

We had looked forward to being with you, meeting Catherine and [the children]—but we will meet another time.

I know Henri would appreciate your prayers, Tim.

Love,

Fred,

I.P.O.Y. (I'm Proud of You) F

A day later, Fred sent me an autographed copy of Nouwen's newest book, Can You Drink the Cup? His accompanying note sounded uncharacteristically melancholy.

We want you to have one of these signed copies. (I had hoped to get you something personally inscribed when we got together with Henri in Chicago, but of course his heart cancelled that trip for all of us.)

[Nouwen's assistant] Sister Sue Mosteller called this morning to say that Henri had been moved from ICU to [the] Cardiac Care Unit, so that's a good sign. The MD says "slight heart attack with some heart damage."

We had a visit with John Costa (our musical director on Mister Rogers' Neighborhood] last evening. His liver is giving him a lot of trouble. He hopes to be able to make the October-November studio schedule. His MD told me that he doubts it very much . . .

So...

We pray and continue to do our work, counting on God's grace to give each of us enough light to take the next steps of the journey.

Joanne and I send our love to you, Catherine, Patrick and Melanie. IPOY, Fred

On September 21, 1996, a sunny Saturday morning, I had settled in with a cup of coffee and the sports page when the telephone rang in our suburban Texas home. When I answered, I was surprised to hear Fred's voice at the other end of the line. Within a few seconds I could tell that my friend was weeping.

"Tim, I just heard that Henri died this morning in Holland," Fred said. "I had to talk to someone who understands how I feel."

During our brief conversation, I told Fred how sorry I was. But as self-centered as it seems, I was also consciously aware of my gratitude. For months, Fred had listened as I had poured out my tattered heart. Now he trusted me enough to reveal his own. I had never been paid such a compliment. I realized that morning that ours was a truly reciprocal friendship. When we said good-bye that morning, I immediately sat down to write.

Sept. 21, 1996 Dearest Fred,

The mystery of life deepens. It has only been a few minutes since you called with the terribly sad news about Henri, and the thoughts and feelings are swirling about, as they do at a time like this.

I would have sworn I would have met Henri Nouwen someday. I felt it was almost fated—the way his writings resonated with me, our mutual friendship with you, his many fans in Fort Worth and his occasional visits here. Several times, after being particularly moved by his writings, I almost wrote to him myself in Toronto to tell him how much his work, his struggle, his love, meant to me. I hate to admit this, but I didn't write because I was sure he received thousands of letters, and even if he read mine, it wasn't likely to make much of an impression. How typically self-centered of me! Now, of course, the opportunity is gone.

I don't know about this business of life and death, Fred. I guess the older I get, the more I realize that I'm not meant to know. Goodness is no guarantee of a long, abundant life, and in my limited human comprehension, that seems so unfair.

But then, this morning, I am blessed to share in the grief and pain of a dear friend like you, knowing that the life and work of Henri is so much alive in the relationship of you and me. And I come to realize that love and goodness are indestructible, utterly indestructible, cannot be reduced by time or death, or any other barriers we humans attempt to impose on those sacred things.

Yes, this life is fragile, and at times, terribly hard. One of the things that most drew me to Henri's writings was his willingness to be vulnerable with his readers, to share not only his joy, but his pain and human brokenness. As you know, I, too, struggle with that brokenness on a daily basis.

But life is good. Shortly after we hung up this morning, as I was sitting in a chair contemplating the news about Henri, I heard the song of a bird, very loud through our open windows on a beautiful, sunny morning. That bird has probably been singing outside my window for eternity, but it took such a reminder of life's fragility for me to finally listen. Not long after hearing the bird, Patrick came bounding into the room to share the joy he felt with a toy he bought yesterday with his own money. I asked him for a hug, and he complied with all the vigor a five-year-old can muster. Fragility, mystery, unspeakable beauty.

I'm glad I was home this morning to share your pain. Thank you for calling. In one of your letters, you put it better than I ever could. "Real friendships work both ways. Your trust confirms my trustworthiness, your love, my loving." Hence, this is a bittersweet day for me—the day the world lost Henri Nouwen in the flesh, and the day I heard a bird sing outside my window on a spectacular autumn morning, the day a true friendship deepened even more.

Catherine is also an admirer of Henri's work, and she sends her love and concern to you in this time of sorrow.

I close with something that will be familiar to you [from Ralph Waldo Emerson's "Friendship"].

". . . The moment we indulge our affections, the earth is metamorphosed; there is no winter, and no night, all tragedies, all ennuis vanish—all duties even, nothing fills the proceeding eternity but the forms all radiant of loving persons. Let the soul be assured that somewhere in the universe it should rejoin its friend, and it would be content and cheerful alone for a thousand years..." *God bless you and yours. All my love, Tim*

9/30/96 My Dear Tim,

Your phone message and your magnificent letter greeted me when I returned from [Henri's memorial service in] Toronto. Thank you for your loving concern. I feel your strong arms upholding us all.

Of course, I thought of you at the service. There were—oh so many—people from all over the world. Henri was continuing to "make connections" even (especially) from heaven. We'll talk about that service some day in person. I thought you might like to have a copy of the bulletin.

My love is with you, my love and deep gratitude. IPOY.
Fred.

10/18/96 Dear Tim,

There's so much to thank you for. Your flowers grace our entrance so I can see them every time I go home. (We had them in the office for the first days, then I wanted to share them with Joanne.) We all thank you for your loving kindness.

Your 10/14 letter is a treasure. You speak your heart in such glorious ways. When you say, "I can offer only my love and my friendship" I wonder if you realize that you're offering the greatest gift I could ever receive.

And what a marvelous story about Henri and Richard. [I had told Fred about how, during a visit to Fort Worth, Nouwen had met a young man named Richard who was in the midst of a divorce. Seeing the pain in his

61

face, Nouwen immediately went to Richard, embraced and consoled him.]
Isn't it miraculous how God uses us (our faces and our hands) to make a
difference? Richard's receiving Henri's embrace would have been a gift to
Henri, too. You know how we say "It works both ways!"

There is so much good waiting to be found in this life. I'm very grateful
to have found you. Love to Catherine, Melanie and Patrick. As always.
IPOY, Fred

Fred and I spoke about Nouwen on the telephone a few days
after I received that letter. He described how hundreds of people,
many of them well known and powerful, had filled the church for
the priest's memorial service. But the most poignant part of the
service, Fred said, were the songs of the mentally handicapped
people with whom Nouwen had lived for so long. Then, over the
telephone, Fred read something Henri had written a few months
before he died.

Within a few years I will be no longer on this earth. The thought of this
does not frighten me but fills me with a quiet peace. I am a small part of life,
a human being in the midst of thousands of other human beings. It is good to
be young, to grow old and to die. It is good to live with others, and to die with
others. . . What counts are not the special and unique accomplishments in life
that make me different from others, but the basic experiences of sadness and
joy, pain and healing, which make me part of humanity. The time indeed is
growing short for me, but the knowledge sets me free to prevent mourning from
depressing me and joy from exciting me.

Mourning and joy can now both deepen and quiet my desire for the day
when I realize that the many kisses and embraces I received today were
simply incarnations of the eternal embrace of the Lord himself.

"Isn't that lovely?" Fred said when he had finished.

Chapter 6

May 1997 was the beginning of an eventful spring and summer. That month I ruptured my Achilles tendon playing pickup basketball. A few weeks later, I was infuriated to learn that co-workers at the newspaper had gained access to private computer files that contained my salary, project proposals, and other personal information. As a result, my personal affairs had become the topic of widespread office gossip.

In our correspondence that spring, Fred told me he was sorry to learn of my injury, which resulted in two painful months on crutches.

"[And] I grieve with you about the invasion of your privacy," Fred wrote when I told him. "You're such an honorable man, consequently you expect that in others. Of course, after the grieving will come the forgiveness (the only thing that evil—Evil—can not stand.)"

Then, in early July, I learned that I had been selected to receive the first Batten Medal, a national award for "excellence and humanity in journalism" that honored James K. Batten, a well-known newspaper executive from Florida who had recently died of cancer. I gave a short speech during the Batten ceremony in the *Star-Telegram* newsroom, and sent a videotape of the event to Fred.

"That speech of yours at the Batten award is so eloquent, so human," Fred wrote when he had watched it. "I'm exceedingly impressed and moved. What I wrote down as I listened was,

'We're journalists; we're not stenographers. We have a duty to let our outrage show through when we come across injustice. We need to let our compassion show through for other people's suffering. And we need to let our Ahhh [awe] show through at the glory of life . . . We have as much responsibility to celebrate life and the goodness of it as we do to root out evil.'

"All I could think of as I heard you speak those truly magnificent sentences was: That sounds like a twentieth-century Jesus talking.' Bravo, Tim. You honored the prize givers. Please believe me. Much love and admiration. Fred."

But the highlight of my summer came later that month, on Tuesday, July 22, when I saw Fred in person for the first time since our meeting in Pittsburgh nearly two years earlier. While visiting Catherine's family in a suburb of Detroit, I decided to take a few days and make the five-hour drive east, emerging from the tunnel through the mountain to see the city by the river once again, and the Cathedral of Learning, at Pitt, and the other places that for me had come to have so much meaning.

Fred and I embraced when we met at his office. Then, because he was tied up at work, I went to lunch with his producer, Margy Whitmer, and David Newell, known to generations of children as Mr. McFeely, the Speedy Delivery man from Mister Rogers' Neighborhood. Fred and I met for a long conversation in his office later that afternoon, and another during a leisurely dinner at an Italian restaurant that evening.

At first I had been somewhat anxious about seeing him again (he was Mister Rogers, after all), but the words flowed freely between us from the beginning. Though there is much about that special night I don't remember specifically, I know we talked at length about the life and writing of Henri Nouwen, about the mystery of death, and about the nature of the sacred. ("The older I get, the more I feel this is true," Fred said. "There's a loving mystery at the heart of the universe, just yearning to be expressed.") I shared more of the healing insights I had gained about my father. He told me how his own father had wept at the death of Fred's grandfather. "Allowing me to see him cry was a great gift to me," Fred said. "It gave me permission to shed my own tears." Fred also spoke that night about his beloved Grandfather McFeely, "who used to tell me, 'Freddy, I love you just the way you are.'"

It was while discussing my recent work that I brought up that spring's disastrous flooding in Grand Forks, North Dakota. I had grown up only twenty-five miles away, just across the border in Minnesota, and had attended college in that small northern city. Shortly after the flood-waters had receded that spring, I flew from Texas to Grand Forks to write a newspaper story about the natural disaster that had completely inundated the place, victimizing many of my oldest and closest friends. While there, I also heard the afflicted people speculate about the identity of the "Angel" who had anonymously donated millions of dollars to Grand Forks flood relief. The local newspaper eventually exposed the benefactress as Joan Kroc, the McDonald's hamburger heiress, who lived in San Diego. Kroc also happened to be a close friend of Fred, he told me that night at dinner, a very humble person who was embarrassed when her identity became known in Grand Forks. I told Fred that there probably could be worse things.

"I heard this somewhere, and I think it's probably true," I said that night. "Few things in life are more pleasurable than doing a good deed anonymously and being discovered accidentally."

Fred grinned.

"I'll have to share that with Joan," he said.

Fred ordered ice cream for our dessert, then insisted on paying for dinner. As we left the restaurant, he grinned.

"I have an idea," he said. "Let's go surprise Joanne."

After a short ride in his small Honda, we rode the elevator in his multi-story apartment building up several floors, and knocked at his door until Joanne answered, dressed in her bathrobe.

"Well, what have you two boys been up to?" she said, laughing.

Their apartment was spacious and warm but without pretense, notable mostly for the two grand pianos that sat at the far end of the living room to accommodate both Fred and his wife, who is a concert pianist. When we had visited for a few minutes, Fred pulled out his camera, grinning. Joanne and I dutifully posed.

Fred had secured a room for me that night at the Pittsburgh Athletic Club, where he was a member, and the next morning at seven there was a knock at my door. When I groggily answered, he stood there beaming, looking fresh and obviously rested, his bow tie crisply affixed to his pressed white shirt.

"Good morning, my dear," he said. "Did you rest well? I thought you might want to join me for a swim."

I had always hated to swim, but didn't have the heart to say so then. So Fred led me into the club's locker room, introduced me to the attendant and a few of his other friends, found me a swimsuit that would fit, then quickly and unselfconsciously stripped off his clothes. On the way to the pool with a towel over his shoulder, he stepped on a locker room scale and smiled.

"One-four-three," he said. "I've weighed exactly one hundred and forty-three pounds for as long as I can remember. Did you know that in sign language that means, 'I love you'? One finger for I; four fingers for love; three fingers for you. Isn't that wonderful?"

He was out the door to the pool before I could answer, and I limped after him, still slowed by my injured ankle. Fred donned a swimming cap and a pair of goggles, grinning at me in that altered appearance before he dove into the water and, in long, graceful strokes, made his way to the other end and back, over and over and over again for a half hour. I tentatively let myself in, made a few laps in a plodding dog paddle, then sat on the side of the pool to watch my friend glide happily through the water.

Later, after we showered, Fred and I ate breakfast together in the brown-paneled dining room of the club. He pulled out his camera and took a photograph of our waiter, who then obliged us by taking a snapshot of Fred and me.

As we ate, I asked him about a starfish curio I had seen in his apartment the night before. Funny I should have noticed that, Fred said. It was a gift from Joan Kroc.

"Is it really?" I said. "Have you ever heard the starfish story?"

"I don't believe I have," Fred said.

"It goes something like this," I said.

After a huge storm, a man walked alone on a beach where thousands of starfish had been washed up onto the sand. In the distance, he saw another man bending to grab something, then hurling whatever it was back into the water. When the first man grew closer, he saw that the second man was gathering starfish, one by one, and throwing them back into the sea.

"What on earth are you doing?" the first man said.

"If these starfish don't get back into the water, they'll die," the second man answered.

"But there are thousands of starfish on this beach," the first man said. "What possible difference could it make?"

"To this one," the second man said, looking down at the starfish he held in his hands, "it makes all the difference in the world."

"Isn't that wonderful," Fred said when I finished. "That one starfish."

Fred insisted I stop by his office after breakfast, where he dug into a closet and came out with a Neighborhood Trolley for my son, and T-shirts for my daughter and other relatives back in Michigan. For the ride back to Detroit, he gave me the tape of a lecture by Karen Armstrong, a renowned writer on spirituality and religion. When we said good-bye, I told him how much I loved him.

"And me, you," he said. "Remember . . . IPOY."

Fred jotted this note later that same day:

Dear Tim,

I'm so proud of you and, as you know, love you dearly.

Thank you for your grace-filled visit. Fred

Enclosed with the note was that day's message from an inspirational calendar he kept in his office. "Each and every act of kindness done by anyone anywhere," the message read, "resonates out into the world and somehow, mysteriously, and perfectly, touches us all."

"Reminds me of your starfish," Fred scribbled in the margins. "143. Fred."

Several months later, a few weeks before my fortieth birthday, in December, Fred sounded almost giddy when he called me at home.

"I've found the perfect birthday present for you," he said. "It should come in the mail in a few days. Of course I can't give you a hint."

The package from Pittsburgh arrived soon thereafter, and when I opened it, I found a beautiful crystal starfish. That was the same holiday season of my marital crisis, the time when I wrote to Fred with such remorse to confess that I was about to leave my wife. "I will never forsake you," Fred had written in return. In that same extraordinary letter, my friend had also invoked the parable of the starfish.

"When I now look at our starfish (on the hall table) I not only think of Joan who gave it to us, but I think of you who gives it extra special meaning," he wrote. "You told me what a difference it made for that one person to save that one starfish. Well, you and I make a similar difference in each other's lives . . . You are my beloved brother, Tim. You are God's beloved son."

Chapter 7

In March 1998, another package arrived from Pittsburgh, this one containing a copy of the best-selling book *Tuesdays with Morrie: An Old Man, a Young Man and Life's Greatest Lessons*. On an inside page was this message, written in that familiar script, on a yellow Post-it note: "With gratitude to God for our everlasting friendship. Love, Fred."

I was particularly touched to receive it from Fred, a gift suggesting that he, too, saw important parallels between our friendship and that of author Mitch Albom and his college professor Morrie Schwartz. It wasn't just that Fred was an older man and I younger, or that, like Albom, I had been the grateful recipient of so much loving wisdom. I also recognized in my bond with Fred an emotional and spiritual intimacy, vulnerability, honesty, and, above all, an intensity similar to what had been depicted in Albom's classic book.

Morrie Schwartz had been dying of Lou Gehrig's disease when Albom took up his weekly vigil with his former professor, which was what gave their friendship a sense of urgency. Time and words were not to be wasted on the trivial. Fred and I, on the other hand, were separated by 1,500 miles and two busy careers, so each letter, each e-mail message, each minute I could spend with him in person was precious. Not once, for example, did I solicit Fred's opinion about the Pittsburgh Steelers, or wonder whether he had caught the cliffhanger episode on ER. (Fred rarely watched television, for one thing.) We talked instead about

God, about love, family, suffering, mystery, and friendship, particularly friendship. As much as anything, our conversations and correspondence were an ongoing meditation on that topic.

In a 1998 e-mail, Fred shared with me the following Arabian proverb.

A friend is one to whom one may pour out all the contents of one's heart, chaff and grain together, knowing that the gentlest of hands will take and sift it, keep what is worth keeping and, with a breath of kindness, blow the rest away.

"I thought of you when I read the above," Fred concluded. "IPOY."

In another e-mail in the spring of 1998, he wrote that "the past two days of Henri's entries in [Nouwen's book] *Bread for the Journey* has made me think of you ... a lot. I'll type them here for you":

A friend is more than a therapist or confessor, even though a friend can sometimes heal us and offer us God's forgiveness. A friend is that other person with whom we can share our solitude, our silence, and our prayer. A friend is that other person with whom we can look at a tree and say, "Isn't that beautiful," or sit on the beach and silently watch the sun disappear under the horizon. With a friend we don't have to say or do something special. With a friend we can be still and know that God is there with both of us....

. . . There is a twilight zone in our hearts that we ourselves cannot see. Even when we know quite a lot about ourselves—our gifts and weaknesses, our ambitions and aspirations, our motives and our drives—large parts of ourselves remain in the shadow of consciousness. This is a very good thing. We will always remain partially hidden to ourselves. Other people, especially

those who love us, can often see our twilight zones better than we ourselves can. The way we are seen and understood by others is different from the way we see and understand ourselves. We will never fully know the significance of our presence in the lives of our friends. That's a grace, a grace that calls us not only to humility, but to a deep trust in those who love us. It is in the twilight zones of our hearts where true friendships are born.

"Can you see why I might have been thinking of you?" Fred wrote that day. "Hope you have a beautiful day in your neighborhood . . . whatever you may be doing. The world is fortunate to have you in it. IPOY, as you well know . . . and grateful for you. Love, Fred."

By the spring of 1998, my marriage was safely on a healing course, I had gained a new understanding and appreciation for my father, and the worst of my despair and crippling depression had begun to dissipate. These happy developments were the direct consequence of having revealed the twilight zone of my own heart to my friend in Pittsburgh. For much of the rest of that year, Fred and I corresponded nearly every week by e-mail, but the messages were taken up less and less with my suffering, and more with other, happier details of our daily lives.

"While the rest of the world watches Seinfeld, I'm able to sit here and delight in your friendship, via this e-mail," Fred wrote on May 14. "We're ready to go back in the studio again. Neighborhood of Make Believe, here we come!!"

My daughter graduated from high school later that spring, and Fred sent her a trolley as a present. ("Please tell her it came 'speedy delivery,'" he wrote.) In a brief note, Fred mentioned his concern for us during a particularly devastating stretch of Texas heat. When Van Cliburn collapsed during a performance in Fort Worth, Fred wrote, "I'm glad we didn't come. His fainting would have scared us silly." I told him about the joys of camping in the Colorado Rockies with my college roommate. Fred responded from their summer home on Nantucket, an ancient little cabin known as The Crooked House.

"Greetings from Nantucket where everyone is worried about hurricanes," Fred wrote. "I just figure that The Crooked House has been here on this spot for 150 years. I can't imagine [Hurricane] Bonnie taking it (and us) away . . . This little spot, way out in the Atlantic, is truly magical."

One winter night in 1978, a deeply troubled man named Willie Daniel Sr. barged into his home in Fort Worth, shot two of his children to death, wounded two more, and sent his wife and another child scurrying in terror into the night. When I came across old newspaper accounts of that horrible spree, I began to wonder what had become of the survivors, what life would be like with such horrors embedded in their memory. I decided to track them down, and when I did, I learned that, remarkably, all of them had gone on to lead productive, reasonably happy lives. That included Willie Daniel Jr., who, in 1998, was working as an air traffic controller and raising a large family of his own in Cleveland.

That October, I made plans to fly north from Fort Worth to interview him. And since Cleveland was just a few hours from Pittsburgh, I also wrote to Fred, wondering whether he might entertain another visit. I was delighted by his reply.

"Would you be able to come over Friday for dinner and/or Saturday for a swim and lunch?" Fred replied. "What would suit you, Tim? It'll be our annual reunion. Bless your heart."

On a brilliant afternoon in late October, I spent several emotional hours with Willie Daniel Jr., listening to his awful and still vivid memories of that night in his childhood home, and the struggle to come to terms with what had happened in the two decades since. At the end of our talk, I told him I was heading over to Pittsburgh to visit a special friend who had also been inspired by the story of Willie and his family when I told it to him a few days earlier. That friend was Mister Rogers.

"You know Mister Rogers?" Willie Jr. said, incredulous. "Get out of here. My kids watched that guy every morning."

I drove into Pittsburgh a few hours later. Early for my appointment to meet Fred for dinner, I parked my rental car and sprawled out at the top of a hill overlooking a large, grassy area on the campus of Carnegie Mellon University. Students below me were lying on blankets studying, or tossing Frisbees. The sun slid lower in a cloudless sky, and the autumn air was beginning to chill as I looked down the hill, overcome with gratitude at the turn my life had taken. It seemed as if I had been delivered from the Furies directly into this golden afternoon, soon to be sharing sacred time with one of history's greatest humans. If, during my greatest suffering, I had doubted the existence of the divine, I could no longer. That afternoon on the hill, I felt joy.

Fred greeted me happily at his apartment a short time later, then excused himself to finish dressing for dinner, allowing me a few moments to roam about his living room, looking at his books and family photographs. It was then that I first saw the copy of *Esquire* magazine on Fred's coffee table, thinking at first it was some sort of a gag. Why else would the smiling face of Mister Rogers adorn a men's publication with sensibilities just this side of Playboy? But it was no joke. CAN YOU SAY . . . HERO? the headline on the cover read. Inside was a long profile written by Tom Junod, one of the magazine's senior writers.

"What's this?" I asked when Fred emerged from his bedroom.

'That's quite unlike anything that's ever been written about me," Fred said. "I'm very curious to know what you will think of it."

"I can't wait," I said, laughing.

We then drove to meet a group of his friends at a Chinese restaurant near his apartment, where Fred promptly spilled a full glass of water on me and over much of our table.

"Oh my goodness," Fred said, mortified. "I'm so very sorry. Let me clean that up."

At dinner, Fred later insisted that I tell his friends the story of how the surviving Daniel children had overcome the horror of that night in their home and had triumphed over evil. He and I later went for coffee and dessert to the Pittsburgh home of Bill Isler, the president of Family Communications, Inc., and one of Fred's closest friends and most trusted advisers. When we had cleared away the dishes, Fred and Bill offered to give me a nighttime tour of the city. Fred rode in the backseat as Bill drove the three of us to the top of a hill on the far side of the Monongahela River, where we looked down on the city that glistened beneath a sliver of new moon. "It looks like a giant apostrophe in the sky," Fred said.

It was close to midnight by the time we made it back to Fred's apartment. Joanne was traveling at the time, performing in a series of piano recitals, and Fred had invited me to spend the night in their guest room. As we said good night, I took the copy of *Esquire* with me off to bed, keenly curious about what a magazine known for its edginess would do with a subject like Mister Rogers. I soon discovered that even a well-known writer at a prestigious national publication was not immune to Fred's goodness, his "unashamed insistence on intimacy." So much of Junod's encounter with the famous man reminded me of my own first meeting with Fred, down to Fred handing over the telephone so the visiting writer could say hello to Joanne.

. . . And though I tried to ask him questions about himself, he always turned the questions back on me. And when I finally got him to talk about the puppets that were the comfort of his lonely boyhood, he looked at me, his blue eyes at once mild and steady, and asked, "What about you, Tom? Did you have any special friends growing up?"

"Special friends?"

"Yes," he said. "Maybe a puppet, or a special toy, or maybe just a stuffed animal you loved very much. Did you have a special friend like that, Tom?"

"Yes, Mister Rogers."

"Did your special friend have a name, Tom?"

"Yes, Mister Rogers. His name was Old Rabbit."

"Old Rabbit. Oh, and I'll bet the two of you were together since he was a very young rabbit. Would you like to tell me about Old Rabbit, Tom?"

And it was just about then, when I was spilling the beans about my special friend, that Mister Rogers rose from his corner of the couch and stood suddenly in front of me with a black camera in hand. "Can I take your picture, Tom?" he asked. "I'd like to take your picture. I like to take pictures of all my new friends, so that I can show them to Joanne ..." And then, in the dark room, there was a wallop of white light, and Mister Rogers disappeared behind it.

Junod's article went on to describe in rather excruciating detail how Fred looked naked before his swim; Mister Rogers' memorable meeting with Koko the Gorilla; a trip back to Latrobe to visit Fred's boyhood home, and to the cemetery where Fred would eventually be buried. (On that afternoon in the cemetery with Junod, Mister Rogers happily relieved himself behind a bush.) Junod wrote of the day Fred and a friend ducked into a New York City subway car filled with black and Hispanic children riding home from school ". . . and they didn't even approach Mister Rogers for an autograph. They just sang. They sang, all at once, all together, the song he sings at the start of his program, 'Won't You Be My Neighbor?' and turned the clattering train into a single, soft, runaway choir."

But the *Esquire* passage I found most poignant and revealing was this one: Mister Rogers' visit to a teenage boy severely afflicted with cerebral palsy and terrible anger. One of the boy's few consolations in life, Junod wrote, was watching Mister Rogers' Neighborhood.

At first, the boy was made very nervous by the thought that Mister Rogers was visiting him. He was so nervous, in fact, that when Mister Rogers did visit, he got mad at himself and began hating himself and hitting himself, and his mother had to take him to another room and talk to him. Mister Rogers didn't leave, though. He wanted something from the boy, and Mister Rogers never leaves when he wants something from somebody. He just waited patiently, and when the boy came back, Mister Rogers talked to him, and then he made his request. He said, "I would like you to do something for me. Would you do something for me?" On his computer, the boy answered yes, of course, he would do anything for Mister Rogers, so then Mister Rogers said: "I would like you to pray for me. Will you pray for me?" And now the boy didn't know how to respond. He was thunderstruck . . . because nobody had ever asked him for something like that, ever. The boy had always been prayed for. The boy had always been the object of prayer, and now he was being asked to pray for Mister Rogers, and although at first he didn't know if he could do it, he said he would, he said he'd try, and ever since then he keeps Mister Rogers in his prayers and doesn't talk about wanting to die anymore, because he figures Mister Rogers is close to God, and if Mister Rogers likes him, that must mean that God likes him, too.

As for Mister Rogers himself... he doesn't look at the story the same way the boy did or I did. In fact, when Mister Rogers first told me the story, I complimented him on being smart—for knowing that asking the boy for his prayers would make the boy feel better about himself—and Mister Rogers responded by looking at me first with puzzlement and then with surprise. "Oh heavens no, Tom! I didn't ask him for his prayers for him; I asked for me. I asked him because I think that anyone who has gone through challenges like that must be very close to God. I asked him because I wanted his intercession."

Finally, in the *Esquire* profile was the story of Fred taking a New York City cab to Penn Station to film a segment of Mister Rogers' Neighborhood with the famous architect Maya Lin. A crowd gathered around him immediately when he stepped onto the sidewalk. 'There was Mister Rogers putting his arms around someone, or wiping the tears on someone's cheek, or passing around the picture of someone's child, or getting on his knees to talk to a child," Junod wrote. And in the crowd were a group of New York mooks, one of whom said, "It's Mister [Freakin'] Rogers!"

I laughed out loud when I read that, lying there long after midnight in Mister Rogers' own guest bedroom. The next morning, when Fred asked me what I thought of the article, I replied that, while certainly different from any I had read, it was very poignant, and had captured him well. He seemed genuinely relieved.

"Can you believe it, Tim," Fred said. "Mister [Freakin'] Rogers."

Fred did not drink coffee, and I could not begin my day without it, so he rummaged around in his cupboards and found a jar of instant. We shared bowls of bran cereal at a little table in his kitchen. Two stories from that breakfast together stand out in my memory, though I can't remember how they came up. One concerned my newspaper assignment several years earlier, at the Texas border with Mexico, where thousands of Central American refugees had come flooding across the Rio Grande, hoping to enter the United States before federal immigration policies became more restrictive. One late afternoon, I hopped into the back of a Ryder rental truck crammed with men, women, and children from the war-torn countries of El Salvador and Nicaragua, people who, in many cases, had walked north across

Mexico and now owned only the clothes they wore. An American church worker had rented the truck to drive them to Houston, a journey lasting several hours. As we sped north up the highway, my legs often dangled over the edge of the open back because the truck was so full. I told Fred that late at night, when the refugees had grown quiet, the beautiful tenor voice of a man singing a folk song in Spanish swept over the truck. Then there was a tap at my shoulder and when I turned around, one of the refugees had pulled his daughter onto his lap so I would have a place to lie down and sleep.

"The man had nothing, but he did that for me, one who had everything," I said to Fred.

"Isn't grace a mystery?" said Fred. (He would go on to use parts of that story in a speech he gave a few weeks later.)

The other memorable story from that morning was Fred's. At a Hollywood function some time earlier, he had been on the dais with several other celebrities, including the comedian Drew Carey, who regaled the audience with his vulgar comedy routine.

Fred said, "I was wondering, 'What can I say to these people after listening to something like that?'"

What Fred did was begin his own speech in his customary way. He asked his audience, people who had been rolling at Carey's raunchy humor only seconds earlier, to take precisely one minute and remember all those who had "loved them into being. I'll time you on my watch," Fred said.

So the room fell silent.

"Within a few seconds I could hear sniffles in the audience," Fred said, sounding mystified by the experience. "Isn't that amazing?"

We swam together again that morning, and had lunch. He later showed me a little office where he did most of his writing. The next morning, at his Bible study class, Fred again asked me to share the story of the Daniel family from Fort Worth. As I left his church for the Pittsburgh airport, my heart had never been so full.

"Welcome home, Tim," Fred wrote in an e-mail message to me that night. "How good it was to be with you. Once again: IPOY!! Love, Fred."

Looking back, it was as if I had been fortified by his love for the tragic journey soon to begin.

Chapter 8

The black-and-white photograph was taken around 1960: two boys who are little more than toddlers, standing side by side and squinting into the Minnesota summer sun, with serious looks on their chubby faces. That's me on the right, just shy of a year older than my brother Steve, and taller by a tad as the two of us stand ankle-deep in the grass of a front lawn. We both wear tennis shoes and are both without shirts, our white skin fluorescent in the sun, our bellies sticking out over the striped shorts our mother had dressed us in that day. But our hands and arms are what make that photograph particularly precious, and whenever I study it today, as I often do, that's where my eyes immediately focus. My right arm rests lightly on my brother's shoulders; Steve's left hand is touching my back, like we were conjoined in some way, two little boys who were a package deal in our small-town Midwestern boyhood.

And so we were. It was said around our house and in our neighborhood that Tim-and-Steve was like one word because we were so often together. I was the timid, introspective one, the reader. Steve was fearless, gregarious, and always into some mischief, be it decorating the walls of my parents' bedroom with lipstick, or going poop in a toy dump truck just as several nuns walked up our sidewalk for a visit. Yet as different as we were, Steve was the boyish heart of my heart, my constant companion and best friend, the guy who always had my back as we grew up on the baseball fields and hockey rinks of the little town called Crookston.

The memories of those games with Steve are almost endless. When I was on the pitcher's mound, he guarded first base. When I stayed back on defense in hockey, he was rushing the puck as a forward. I can still see our bright red uniforms from one such game when we were in junior high, can smell the ice, can see the grandstands of the arena where our youth hockey team was playing. The game went into overtime, which was when I passed the puck to Steve, and his shot was the winning goal. But what I remember most was what happened next, flying into his arms in celebration, just the two of us embracing in that moment, a sensation of joy and brotherly love that was almost painful in its intensity.

Yet the true magic of our shared boyhood was not found in those moments of euphoria, but quietly hidden from view in the basement room where our bunk beds were stacked. For thousands of nights we lay together in that room, talking in dusky voices until one or the other could talk no more, and only then would we say good night and finally drift off to sleep. Summer nights with Steve were the best, when we'd have our bedroom windows open to catch the cool breeze, curtains would billow, and the sound of our voices would mix with the shimmering leaves of a mammoth cottonwood tree just outside.

How I wish I could relive just one of those late-night talks, could hear again exactly what it was we discussed. I only know now that we talked about everything—girls, teachers, the future, family, life, death, friends, sports, God—that young souls were revealed. And though I can't recall his specific words, as I lay listening to Steve from the top bunk I marveled even then that a boy so frenetic and adventurous on the outside could be so deep and tender within. So we talked and talked and talked to each other, never lonely as a result, never alone in our boyhood fears, because from the time we were little until we had both graduated from college and left home for good, my brother Steve and I shared the night.

It was just a few years ago that I took my son back to Crookston, showing him where I went to school, where I played ball, the yellow house on Alexander Street where we lived when I was a boy. By that time, my parents had long since retired and moved to the Twin Cities to be closer to my other brothers and sisters, so some other family lived in the yellow house. There was no answer when I knocked at the front door that Minnesota evening with my son, so I took the liberty of leading Patrick around to the back, and we knelt to peer together through the basement windows into the place that had been our room, which was now strewn with the toys of other children. Then my son and I stood beneath the Cottonwood that had survived through the decades.

"Does this make you watery eyed?" Patrick, who was eleven at the time, asked me that night.

"Yes," I said. "I guess it does."

"Why are we standing under this tree?" Patrick asked.

"I'm listening for the sound of the leaves," I said.

"But, Dad, there's no wind," Patrick said. "I don't think you're going to hear them."

I smiled at my son. "I hear them, all right," I said.

It is remarkable and tragic to think that the brotherly bond of Steve and me did not survive into adulthood. I graduated from the University of North Dakota in 1980 with a degree in journalism. Steve finished a year or so later with a business degree from the same school, married young and quickly divorced, worked as a manager for Kmart, and had two boys with his second wife. If anything, he became even more frenetic as the years went by, abandoning the relative security of the corporate world to form his own commercial cleaning business, first in the suburbs of Chicago, then in Davenport, Iowa. It was a business that sank progressively deeper into debt.

Meanwhile, I sought to tame my own Furies with a single-minded pursuit of recognition in the newspaper world. That quest took me to Texas, the only one of my parents' seven children to leave the Midwest. I realize now that the extent of my self-preoccupation was such that I had little real use for those who could not immediately benefit me, and sadly, when I moved away, that included my brother. While Steve and I would occasionally see each other during holidays over the years, we rarely spoke otherwise, and what was left of our relationship broke down completely one night in late 1992.

During a rare visit to see him, and after too much beer, Steve confronted me that night in his Chicago apartment. In a mounting rage, he accused me of betraying him and our family with my ambition and self-centeredness, and by moving so far away. For a few dreadful minutes we seemed on the verge of blows. I grabbed my suitcase instead and pushed by him out the door to find a hotel. Steve and I mumbled apologies to each other on the telephone the next day, and promised to talk soon, but it would be years before I again heard the sound of his voice.

In 1997, when our family gathered for Thanksgiving in Minneapolis, Steve and I tried to mend things, heading off alone to sit and talk in the bar of an Olive Garden restaurant. I apologized for my selfishness and thoughtlessness. He told me how dependent on me he had been when we were young, that he had felt lost when I went away, and that he was still trying to learn to stand on his own two feet. We pledged that night to put the past behind us, to try and start our relationship anew. But I think Steve and I both knew they were just words even as we said them. I began to reconcile myself to the fact that the chasm between us might always remain.

By the time of my youngest sister's wedding the following September, my own Furies were finally in retreat. But when I saw him that weekend, Steve was thin and pale and consumed with fear, anger, and bitterness. Though he had always been a devoted, loving father to his two sons, his marriage clearly was in trouble. There seemed no way out of his business woes. By then, Steve was working up to fifteen hours a day, largely because he didn't want to be at home. He was chain-smoking and drinking too much. I wanted to reach out to him that weekend at the wedding, to help him if I could, but I was fairly certain that I was the last person he would listen to.

Then, later that fall, Steve consulted a doctor, complaining of chronic hoarseness. On November 4, 1998, my mother called me at my newspaper desk to tell me that X-rays showed a golf ball-sized tumor on Steve's aorta, what doctors believed was an aggressive form of lung cancer that would probably be inoperable because of its location.

After hanging up with Mom, I called my wife to give her the news, then took a long walk along the Trinity River in Fort Worth. I remember that it was a misty autumn day, but otherwise my mind was blank from the shock. Back in the office, I called Fred's home number in Pittsburgh, and could not finish my first sentence when I heard the voice of his wife, Joanne, on the other end of the line. My sadness and shock, multiplied by my guilt, spilled out as Joanne quietly consoled me. She sent an e-mail message later that afternoon.

"Prayers are surrounding all you Madigans and I know God hears us!" Joanne wrote. "Tim, I'm sorry I couldn't reach out from the phone to hold you and comfort you in your grief— and share it with you—but I hope you know how much we care for you and yours. I phoned Fred and shared your news with him, so you know he'll be there for you whenever you need him! Me too! . . . Love, Joanne (Rogers, that is)

Fred's own message arrived an hour later.

Joanne called me after her talk with you a little while ago. She thought you might have been calling from home, so I tried reaching you there. Catherine answered. That must have been providential. She and I had a wonderful talk . . . at last. I'm so glad to have had the chance to hear her voice and her positive attitude about what your brother is going through right now. She said he had received his medical news as a blessing rather than a curse. All I can say is that you Madigan men are certainly mighty special guys.

All morning I had been thinking of you. Long before Joanne called, Toni (the woman who takes care of the "care packages" as you call them) had left a note on my chair asking me to sign two little trolleys for Philip, age 6, and Abbee, age 3. And the next part of her note was what made my mind travel at lightning speed to you. Here's what she wrote about those children: "They are the ones whose father shot their mother in front of them." All I could think of was, "Just like twenty years ago in Fort Worth."

Tim, my heart leaps to you as you bear your sadness about Steve's illness. You can be assured of our prayers. Who you are and what you mean to Steve and his family is something that neither time nor space can ever take away. They (as well as all of us who love you) are truly blessed to have you in their lives. Hope to talk with you soon. Love, Fred

So it was, from that day forward, that Fred and his wife joined hands with Steve and the rest of our family in the fight for my brother's life, and in the struggle to find meaning in terrible suffering. Every morning before the sun came up, Fred prayed for Steve by name, and for his wife, Cally, for their two young sons, Timmy and Tyler, for my parents, and for me. But he did much more than pray. Through dozens of e-mail messages, gifts, letters, and telephone calls, Fred became one of us, rejoicing as Steve grew into a man of spiritual greatness himself, and suffering with our family with each medical setback.

I received his e-mail message just after 6:00 AM on Thanksgiving Day, just a few weeks after my brother's diagnosis. It read: "I'm thankful for YOU, Tim. Thinking about all the Madigan family today. If you talk with Steve, please give him greetings from the Rogers family."

Then, of course, he signed off in his customary way.

IPOY. Love, Fred

Chapter 9

I spoke with Steve by telephone the day after his diagnosis and knew immediately that something about him had changed.

"I've never been more scared in my life," he told me then. "But in some ways, I've never been more peaceful, either. It's not about the cancer, but about the good that I can make come out of it."

But as much as his remarkable words, it was the tone of his voice that was revealing. In place of his characteristic frenzy and recent bitterness was a deep calm that reflected an almost instant transformation, one that my family will always consider something of a miracle.

"He went from being completely alone," my brother Pat would say years later, "to someone who had everything in the world he ever wanted. He told me it was the best thing that had ever happened to him. He said, 'I'd rather live two years like this, than a lifetime the way things were before.'"

It happened the day after his initial diagnosis. Until then, Steve had spent his time working, or coaching the sports teams of his son Timmy, or watching television in his basement while Cally kept her distance upstairs. For reasons only they would know, a great wall of discontent had grown up between them and it seemed only a matter of time before their marriage would end. But the day of his diagnosis, Cally came down the stairs to express her love and concern. Steve felt a strange peacefulness that day and slept through the night for the first time in months.

Then, the following morning, he did not want to leave home. He and his wife began to talk, and in a heartbeat their relationship was transformed from one of rancor to a bond of deep caring and love.

My mother told me later that Steve called her that night and said, "Mom, you're never going to believe what happened."

"Steve and Cally sat down together with their coffee and they talked for hours," my mother told me. "They cried together. They started talking and somehow realized they didn't want to get a divorce. A peace came over both of them. Steve said Cally felt it, too. It was like a million pounds had been lifted off their shoulders. He said it was a truly religious experience, truly a God experience."

On November 13, Steve and Cally received biopsy results that confirmed the worst: His tumor was a rapidly growing form of lung cancer that was inoperable. My parents were visiting in Davenport at the time, and when Steve and his wife had returned home from the oncologist's office with that terrible news, my mother handed Steve a copy of a little pamphlet called *Living Faith*, a monthly publication of the Roman Catholic Church that, with her Bible, was part of her daily spiritual reading. The *Living Faith* message for that day spoke of a grain of wheat, put into the ground by the farmer. Steve was awestruck by the timeliness of the little parable, reading it while standing by his dining room table.

If the grain of wheat could know fear, it would be paralyzed with anxiety at the thought of being dropped in the ground, covered over, put out of sight, doomed to inactivity, yet what a glorious harvest awaits it.

Although we merely project fear onto a grain of wheat, we know for sure that we have real fears. Fear of the unknown. Fear of not being in control at all times. Such fears limit our potential. We accumulate things, ideas, people, holding onto them tight, expecting to be enriched by adding on more and more. All the while, God is whispering gently in our hearts saying;

"Let go, dear one. I want to make something marvelous of you. Loosen up. Drop what is in your hand, your mind, your heart, and let me take over. I love you and have plans for you that pass your wildest imaginings. Only you must let Me be in charge."

Steve had never been an overtly spiritual person before because he had never had time. "He was always racing," as my mother said. But now, faced with the most frightening ordeal humanly imaginable, he would be a grain of wheat ready to surrender himself to the great farmer. He framed the passage from *Living Faith* and kept it near him like a talisman, reading it several times a day. "Okay, loosen up. I've got to loosen up," he would tell himself, over and over.

He soon began to speak with the wisdom of a mystic, describing his cancer as the best thing that had ever happened to him, a blessing that saved his marriage and brought all members of his family closer together. The deep, tender person I remembered from those boyhood nights reemerged. Steve suffered terrible nightmares and was often terrified of dying, particularly late at night when he was alone. But it was then, "in the depths of hell, that I feel closest to God," he told my mother.

"Jubilate Deo. (Praise God)" Fred wrote after one of my regular updates on Steve. "Steve has already known what healing is all about. That's the best kind of all . . . We never know, do we?

93

Every day is a gift to each one of us ... no matter what our present prognosis happens to be. You know that. You write about that in many different ways. Please give him and his family our love when you talk with him."

In another note, Fred wrote, "Steve is now teaching us all."

And so he was—an inspiration to everyone, including his doctors and nurses, with his courage, insight, and faith. But for those of us who loved him, the joy over his spiritual healing was always tempered by the grim reality of his disease. Early on, when I described Steve's diagnosis to an oncologist friend of mine in Texas, my friend's voice turned very grave. "Oh, my," he said. "I'm so sorry." Whether Steve knew from the beginning that he was dying, he never said. But as we all would learn later, inoperable lung cancer is essentially incurable. Treatment available at the time could only hope to prolong life, not save it.

"Didn't sleep last night. Really struggling with this Steve stuff," I wrote in my journal on November 23, 1998. "Seems so unreal that he has cancer—that he might die—seems so unreal that any of us might die."

What's more, in the first year of his illness, Steve and I still struggled with the residue of that terrible night in Chicago in 1992. Most of my information about his condition during that time came secondhand, through my mother. When my brother and I talked on the telephone we were still awkward and tentative. I deeply regret this now, but for many months I did not travel to see him, wondering what my place should be in his treatment, thinking that, because of the old hurts, my presence might actually be a detriment. Then, one day almost a year after his diagnosis, I could wait no longer. I picked up the telephone and called Steve at his home in Iowa.

"I hope you're not busy this weekend," I said, "because I'm coming."

I left before sunrise on a Thursday morning in early November of 1999 for the seventeen-hour drive from Fort Worth to Davenport, choosing not to fly because the drive would give me more time to pray, which I did for much of the long trip north. It was early evening when I called Steve from somewhere in Missouri, telling him I was still several hours away. I could hear the tension in his voice when he answered.

About 10:00 PM I finally pulled up to his home in a quiet Davenport neighborhood, and found that the long hours of praying must have worked; I never felt a second of unease from the moment I took Steve into my arms. He looked wonderful, tall and lean and whole, a handsome man with dark hair and a mustache and the same devilish smirk I had known all my life. I had brought a Dallas Stars hockey jersey for his oldest son, Timmy, who was delighted with the gift, and a Dallas Cowboys jersey for young Tyler, who said he'd rather have the Stars jersey instead. Steve and I shared our first laugh of the weekend at that.

Cally was gone that night, out supervising cleaning crews of the family business, so my brother and I grilled steaks on his deck in back, and sat up through much of the night in his basement. The old hurts never came up. We talked about our sons, instead, amazed to think that they were now the ones growing up on the baseball fields and hockey rinks. For the first time I could remember as an adult, Steve seemed genuinely interested in my life and work, not threatened by it. He also asked several questions about my friendship with Fred.

"We talk about you all the time," I told Steve. "Fred prays for you and Cally and the boys by name every morning. Did you know that?"

"You've got to be kidding me," he said. "Mister Rogers prays for me?"

"Every morning," I said. "I know he does."

"God," Steve said, and his eyes misted over. "That's so awesome."

In fact, so much about his life was awesome, he said. Like the first sip of coffee in the morning, or the sight of the cardinals in the branches near his house, or the goal Timmy scored the other day in hockey. He had never fully appreciated those things before, the little things, he said.

But he was scared, too. His chemotherapy had kept his tumor in check for several months, but recent tests had shown that it was growing again. Steve was hoping to get into an experimental cancer treatment program at the University of Wisconsin that seemed to have great promise, but there were no guarantees that he could. He latched on to the story of cyclist Lance Armstrong's miraculous recovery. But he was also haunted by the recent cancer death of football legend Walter Payton. For himself and his family, Steve would fight his disease with all the faith and courage he could muster. He desperately wanted to live to see his boys grow up and enjoy the new peace and happiness he had found with Cally. But Payton's death was a grim reminder that even the greatest faith and courage were sometimes not enough to survive. And several times during my weekend visit, Steve excused himself, stepping into the bathroom because his chemo made him vomit.

A large, grassy field sprawled down from Steve's deck in back to a little creek, and I spent several hours there with Timmy and Tyler after school on Friday and on Saturday morning, throwing a football, or pushing them on a swing hung from a giant tree. Timmy, who had been named after me twelve years earlier, was a shy, introspective boy much like I had been. Tyler, who was six at the time, was more like his dad as a child, forever on the go and the life of the party. Steve grinned broadly as he watched me play with his sons that weekend. By the time I left on Sunday, it seemed as if I were an uncle who had always lived around the corner.

On Saturday afternoon, we drove to an arena in neighboring Moline, Illinois, where Timmy's hockey team had a game. Steve was also the head coach of the team, so I sat next to Cally and Tyler in the stands, watching as Timmy played and my brother paced back and forth behind the bench, tugging nervously at his hair, yelling instructions to his players as the game went on. Afterward I went down to the locker room and saw how Steve's young players and their parents adored him, which made me very proud and just a little envious.

We had a fine, laughter-filled dinner at a Davenport restaurant that Saturday night, then Steve and I had another talk into the wee hours. But what I remember most from that first trip is a small errand, or what seemed so at the time. On Friday afternoon, just a few minutes before he was due to pick the boys up at school, Steve and I raced toward a hardware store. I remember that we were talking about our days playing hockey together as he pulled up and parked. He sprang from the car, walking at a breakneck pace as he always did, leaning forward as if into a strong wind. In the store he paced up and down in the light fixture section until he found the fixtures he wanted, charged over to the cashier, and paid by credit card. Within five minutes we were off again, headed toward the school, talking about hockey.

I've replayed that errand a hundred times in my head in the years since. Who would ever have thought that a trip to the hardware store could be such a sacred occasion? But it was. Steve was whole and strong and handsome and leaning into the wind as he always did, and he bought his light fixtures during minutes together that we would never have again. That errand with Steve was a great lesson for me: Every second is sacred time, in one way or another. As Fred had said, "Every day is a gift to each one of us ... no matter what our present prognosis happens to be."

I left Steve's very early on Sunday morning for the long drive back to my home in Texas. I was eager to get home, because Patrick was battling a severe case of the flu that would eventually turn into pneumonia. But it was very hard to say goodbye.

"I can't believe how easy this has been," Steve said that morning by my car. "It has just flowed."

I cried for a good many miles heading southwest down an Iowa interstate. I prayed a lot on the way home, too, but this time they were prayers of immense gratitude for the brother who had been lost to me, then found.

Chapter 10

When I was nineteen years old, a popular high school classmate and close friend was killed in a plane crash, which was my first intimate experience with tragedy. It was shattering, but as I grieved at the time, I also marveled how life in our little town otherwise went on as usual. People went to the store and bought groceries as they always had, still filled their cars at the gas pumps, still continued to complain about the Minnesota Vikings, and so on. So it was in 1999, as my brother fought lung cancer. I received reports on his condition every week, thought about him and prayed for him every day, but went on with my life pretty much as usual because in the end the world never stops, even for very difficult things.

And by then, there was little in that life that I did not share with my friend in Pittsburgh. In fact, I began 1999 with Fred's words—the first of dozens of e-mail messages we would exchange that year. It was written a few minutes after 5:00 AM on New Year's Day.

Dear Tim,

Joanne told me that you called yesterday. Thanks so much for your greetings. I'm delighted to hear that Steve is doing well. I think about you all so much . . . and, of course, pray for you daily. You are so close to my heart. I need to tell you this on the first day of this last year before we sail into 2000. I wonder why such things as "millennia" mean so much to people. Maybe we're always looking for some kind of excuse to try big resolutions. . . resolutions that are meant to make things better and better all along the way.

Anyway, just thinking about you gives me joy, Tim. You are certainly one of God's great gifts to me in this life. You are a wonderful person, and, on this New Year's Day, I want you to know all over again; IPOY Love, Fred

Later that January, I made the first of many reporting trips to Ciudad Juarez, Mexico, a teeming city just across the Rio Grande from El Paso, for a series of stories that would be published in the *Star-Telegram* later that year. My series concerned the mysterious murders of dozens of young Mexican women, many of whom had been drawn to Juarez from their villages by the promise of work in American factories that had sprouted up on the south side of the border. But I was also haunted by the Third World poverty that I witnessed then for the first time, miles and miles of cardboard hovels stretching off into the desert, with dirt floors and no indoor plumbing or running water. By contrast, the pristine towers of the University of Texas at El Paso were in plain sight just across a narrow ribbon of the Rio Grande.

Tens of thousands lived in those Juarez slums, but I remember one person in particular, a three-year-old boy named Juan Inez. With his big brown eyes, doughy cheeks, and beautiful olive skin, Juan bore a striking resemblance to another little boy I knew, my nephew Sean, who lived in Minneapolis. I couldn't help comparing the lives of the two. Sean lived in a big house, had his own room, plenty to eat, and was becoming a fine young hockey player. Juan lived in a one-room hut made of tar paper and cardboard. At night he shared a sleeping bag and a dirt floor with two older siblings. Juan drank dirty water from a rusty barrel. He wore a dusty Lion King T-shirt, laughed when I threw him a ball, and stubbornly tried to ride a tricycle without wheels. The day I met him, I emptied my wallet to Juan's mother, and returned to visit several other times that year. In the midst of the pervasive squalor, it occurred to me that Juan was a starfish.

"I guess this note is part of an attempt to make sense of the powerful feelings that I'm struggling with now," I wrote in an e-mail message to Fred in February 1999, after one of my trips to see Juan in Juarez. "Am I weird, unbalanced, to be so deeply affected by this?"

"Oh, Tim, you're the sensitive, caring person you've always been," Fred replied. 'The one who doesn't 'use' people for a story but the one who goes to be 'with' them . . . like Jesus. He could have stood aloof and not cared for the human plight, but He chose to be 'one' with us . . . one of us. I'm so proud of you. How often I say that!! How blessed those children (and the adults who try to care for them) are to have you as their friend."

In that message, Fred went on to describe his own visits to the Third World missions of another friend, Father William Wasson, a Roman Catholic priest who had cared for thousands of children in Mexico, Central America, and Haiti.

"What one person can do in a lifetime!!" Fred wrote. "And you're doing your piece . . . letting others know what it's like in far away back yards of the world. Bless you, my dear friend. F."

A few weeks later, I e-mailed Fred again from my desk at the newspaper, hopelessly mired in writer's block as I tried to compose my stories about Juarez, feeling wholly inadequate to the task and to the subject. Fred's reply popped into my computer minutes later.

"God is up to the task, therefore so are you," he wrote. "Those people are blessed to have your eyes and ears and talents dedicated to their story. I look forward with great anticipation to reading the words of your heart. May you be well blessed in all you do, my friend."

In the weeks to come, Fred's words continued to tide me through one of the most challenging assignments of my newspaper career, even as my friend suffered from his own ailments.

March 13, 1999 6.03 AM Dear Tim,

You are so often in my thoughts. Just wanted you to have this Saturday morning greeting. Hope you've been able to complete the writing of your story from South of the Border. Also hope Steve is faring well. Love to you, as always. Fred

March 26, 1999 3.31 AM

Dear Tim,

Thanks so much for sending your Juarez pieces. No wonder you were so invested in doing such a fine job with that assignment. That's a real ministry you have, Tim. Bless your heart. . . There must be something about this medicine I'm taking for the cough I've been having for three weeks (just started the medicine on Thursday) which makes me wake up almost every hour in the night. At any rate it's a good time to read . . . especially the "Star-Telegram". . . and its star reporter!! Again, my thanks, Tim. Love to all the Madigans, as always, Fred

March 26, 1999 6.04 PM

What a dear man you are, Tim. And how blessed those folks in Juarez are to have you as another of their advocates!! Everybody tells me that "rest is essential" so I've stayed home all of today. I miss my swims, but I'm doing my best to get better so I can complete the taping on Tuesday. Joanne is a wonderful "nurse." Know that I think of you every day. . . and am so grateful for your "presence" in my life.

Love,

Fred

Later that year, in his e-mail message of April 6, 1999, Fred made an impassioned plea for the life of a man he never knew, a tortured World War II veteran named Wendell Smith. "As I finished Chapter 21, I wanted to call out, Tim, Tim, please don't let Wendell die,'" Fred wrote that day.

Indeed, in that particular life-and-death situation, I had some say. Wendell was a character in my first novel that I had completed that spring and shared with Fred before attempting to find a publisher. The book had been a labor of great love, written on weekends and in early mornings over several years, and the book's characters eventually became as real and as dear to me as my own family and friends. I loved Wendell, who was greatly tormented by his memories of the war, and by his part in a secret atrocity. He was sustained and comforted by his wife, a saintly woman named Selma. Wendell's friend, a young woman named Claire, had terrible secrets of her own that she eventually shared with the old man. The book also came to include Van Cliburn's music as a plot device; scenes in which two teenage brothers shared the same room, speaking to each other deep into the night; and pieces of dialogue that I knew Fred would recognize. ("Anything mentionable is manageable," Wendell told Claire, trying to coax out her sorrows.)

As much as I loved the book, at well over two hundred pages I worried that foisting it on Fred would be too much of an imposition. If it was, he concealed it well. Fred wrote on April 6:

Oh, my, Tim, your "people" will be forever with me. I literally wept as Selma was dying . . . And all those references to Van. Won't he be thrilled? Even I was thrilled with the mention of Pittsburgh on page 194 . . .

Ever since I received your manuscript I could hardly wait for my workday to be over so that I could come home and read as many chapters as possible before going to bed. As you can imagine, I just finished reading this mighty special work. I wondered at every passing page how much of you was reflected in it. The main thing that it did, of course, was to make me want to get to know as much as possible about your particular "mentionables." I guess I want to listen to your heart.

He offered criticisms of the novel, too, which I appreciated as much as Fred's praise. In the book, one of my characters played a Rachmaninoff piano concerto without accompaniment, which Fred pointed out can't technically be done. (A sonata, not a concerto, is played in solo recital.) "Also, something I just learned recently (since we did a film for the Neighborhood about people making sidewalks): I always thought it was cement sidewalks, but it's not: it's concrete. Cement is used to make concrete; cement is not used (by itself) to make sidewalks. Of course, all that is minor compared with the development of the theme of Wendell's and

Claire's 'furies.' That is masterfully done. You write so well, Tim."

There was one other criticism, of course, concerning the shotgun blast in the last paragraph that ended Wendell's life.

I wanted a hopeful (Hollywood?) ending. I longed for even further redemption in the life of that tortured man . . . all the while knowing what a difference Selma made . . . what a difference "mentionable is manageable" made. . . and I want you to feel that Wendell has a hopeful future.

Of course, you may let me know that Chapter 21 is indeed NOT the end of the book, that you wanted to see how I would react to it and that you'll soon be sending me "the rest." No matter though, you've passed the test (for me) of great art, you've helped me meet and learn and care for people who are painted by your words on a piece of paper. I find that an extraordinary accomplishment, Tim, and I congratulate you. What an enormous piece of work, beautifully composed. I "explode" with pride knowing how much of your "self" you've shared with your reader.

BRAVO, TIM... BRAVO

IPOY

Love,

Fred

Then, around Thanksgiving that year, I had the chance to share with Fred another piece of recognition, though this of the dubious variety. An alternative local newspaper saw fit to include me among the winners of its annual "Turkey Awards" because of supposed flaws in my Juarez coverage. (Not everyone shared Fred's high opinion of it, evidently.) I sent a copy of the "Turkey Awards" issue to Fred. "I suspect you've been the target of stuff like this," I wrote in the margins. "This is a first for me. Doesn't really bother me that much, but I have a hard time understanding that kind of meanness. I almost feel sorry for people like that. No, do feel sorry for them."

Fred immediately mailed the copy back to me, his own note written in the margins below mine.

"I'm returning this to you," he said. "It's mean-spirited, unkind, and poorly written. What I suggest is that you tear it up and flush it down the toilet (I mean this literally!) It stems from jealousy and evil. I too feel sorry for the 'writers,' but that doesn't condone this turkey crap. IPOY."

I chuckled when I read the word crap. Mister Rogers could talk tough, after all. But for once I did not take Fred's advice, fearing that the article would clog up our plumbing. In any event, given the suffering and heartbreak to come in the next several months, such public ridicule would seem less than a trifle.

My brother was about to embark on the final leg of his amazing odyssey.

Chapter 11

In mid-July of 2000, I sent Fred the cherished photograph of Steve and me as shirtless, nearly conjoined toddlers standing in the Minnesota grass.

"I wanted to share this with you," I wrote to him, "because nothing better illustrates our boyhood bond. But if you could, please return it by certified mail. It's the only copy I have."

By then it was clear how priceless such mementos of my brother would soon become. The previous spring, Steve had made it through the hockey season as coach of Timmy's team, but only through a fierce act of will. He fought hoarseness and terrible chest pain at every game and practice. In late March he found blood in his stool. In mid-April he collapsed while at home alone, suddenly paralyzed, and was forced to crawl to the telephone to call for help. At a Davenport hospital, doctors discovered that Steve's tumor had encircled his spinal cord, prompting emergency surgery to cut out pieces of the invading mass. That allowed Steve to regain feeling in his legs, but doctors said the remedy would be temporary. The tumor would grow back, the paralysis would return, and there was very little doubt, even among the most hopeful of us, what the final outcome would be.

I flew to Davenport the day after learning of his setback, and found Steve smiling up at me from his bed in the hospital. I hugged him and kissed his forehead.

'This sucks, huh," he said.

"Big-time," I said.

"I have a peace about being paralyzed, if that's what it's going to be," Steve said then. "But I don't have a peace about dying. I'm still going to beat this thing."

Steve never would make peace with death. His means of coping was to remain hopeful, focusing his immense spirit on physical healing, no matter what the odds against him. His determination filled the corridors of the hospital that weekend as he tried to relearn how to walk. Steve clutched a metal walker, inching forward down the hallway as my dad held his belt to support him from behind. The rest of us—Cally, Timmy, and Tyler, my mother, my brother Pat, and me— followed along in the rear, speaking encouragement.

Back in the hospital room, Steve and I howled with laughter as Tyler beat me in game after game of cards that we played on the foot of Steve's bed. I rode along that weekend as Cally drove Tyler to his second ever T-ball practice. I'll never forget the sight of the little boy in the front passenger seat, little cap pulled down over his eyes, his little glove and bat next to him. His dad was dying, but on the drive to practice, Tyler's mind was somewhere else. "I hope I get to bat first," he said.

One night at Steve's home in Davenport, Timmy said he felt like he was running a fever, and I had the privilege of taking his temperature and giving him aspirin. My mother, father, and I spent wonderful times together that weekend. I had meaningful talks with my brother Pat, maybe for the first time ever because he is so much younger and was just a boy when I left home.

"Some things about this are so very sad," I wrote in my journal that weekend. "But I can't help but see the blessings in it.

108

Right now, in fact, I don't know whether I'm coming or going; foot or horseback."

Steve wept in his hospital bed when I said good-bye on a Sunday afternoon.

"This has been a new beginning for us," he said. "All because of this darn cancer. Isn't that funny?"

"I still think you and I are going to have long lives together," I said. "I still think we'll watch our kids grow up."

As I flew home to Texas, there was a piece of my heart that still believed it.

My mother, Lois Madigan, worked full-time as a school nurse while raising seven children, did all the laundry and cooking despite suffering from increasingly debilitating arthritis, and somehow managed to remain a woman of indomitable good cheer, a constant source of tenderness, love, and support for my younger siblings and me. Once, while she was folding clothes in the basement, I asked her how she managed to do it all without cracking up.

"Well," she said then, "you just can't lose your sense of humor."

I suspect her quiet but intense faith also had a lot to do with her strength. Most of her life she rose early to have uninterrupted time to pray and read the Bible, savoring those quiet moments in the morning with God and a cup of coffee. And it must have taken every ounce of my mother's preternatural optimism, every ounce of her faith, to sustain her through those terrible weeks when Steve's life dwindled away. But she endured with quiet humor, dignity, and love, and was a tremendous source of comfort to my brother at all hours of the day. Once, as my mother sat by Steve's hospital bed, he stared at her hands that were twisted and swollen from the arthritis.

"What are you looking at, Steve?" my mother asked him.

"Healing hands," my brother replied.

My parents never left Davenport after Steve's legs began to fail him, staying to help with the boys and help care for Steve, particularly when Cally was away from home to supervise the cleaning crews. Often, when Steve woke late at night, panting from nightmares, it would be my mother who would go to comfort him. As the days passed, she began to make notes in the margins of her Bible, or on pieces of scrap paper, trying to capture each sacred moment. Her words, rendered then from the heart of suffering, will echo across subsequent generations of my family.

. .. When Steve was still able to walk we'd parade down the hall to bed, Steve with his walker, Kirby [the golden retriever] at his side, me, Timmy, Tyler, Dad and Cally if she was home. Many nights Timmy would have the bed made with the covers folded diagonally back and fresh water and the [television] remote on his [bed]stand. Tyler would take off his socks and shoes. Kirby would go to the corner of the bed. Tyler would give him the "goodnight, dude" sign and the "I love you" sign. Most nights they said the [Lord's Prayer]. In the morning, Timmy would love to make his dad breakfast before he went to school, six scrambled eggs with four pieces of toast and coffee. He'd just be in there tearing up the kitchen . . .

. . . Some nights were very good for Steve and on these nights he tried to stay awake to enjoy no pain, no anxiety. Other nights were long. "My mind takes me to places that I don't want to go," he said. If Cally was working,

we'd leave our door open in case he needed us. One night he woke from a bad dream and was so afraid. He asked me to sit with him until he fell asleep. He cried so hard that night and tried so hard to get ahold of himself. "Okay. Okay. Relax. Relax," he'd say. He didn't say what the dream was about, only that it was terrifying and dark. I'd hold his hand or touch his arm and sit quietly until he said he was okay and drifted back to sleep. Most times we would sit for a while and we'd chat about the kids, God and his power. "I'm not in charge," he'd say. . .

. . . .He loved his coffee in the morning. He was always so polite. It was always, "Please. Thank you. No thank you ..." One day, Cally was talking about work when Steve [by that time his hospital bed was in the living room] stopped her cold. "Stop, Cally. Look at that bird outside the window." She looked at him with surprise. That was what he was beginning to appreciate. . .

. . . We had wonderful times at ballgames watching Timmy. We could park on a hill [where we could] see the whole diamond. I know there were times when he didn't feel like it, but he didn't miss any. (We couldn't watch Tyler at his games because there wasn't any parking where we could see the field, and Steve couldn't walk to the bleachers.) I remember the pride on Steve's face when Timmy made a diving catch in the outfield. Then he'd say, "Just think, Timmy is doing this all on his own. I'm not there to help him out.. ."

. . . One evening I was sitting with him and remembered how when he was six or seven he told me when he grew up he was going to build a house right next to us so he could stay close to us. He remembered, smiled and said, "Now we're almost in the same room. Isn't that crazy?" He said, "Just think, Dad and I butted heads all the while I was growing up and now he can't get close enough to me." Steve wouldn't go anywhere without his dad, in or out of the house.

. . . After he had his MRI on June 23, the doctor told us the bad news. The tumor had spread throughout the chest area and [there was] more spine involvement. One day, about four days after coming home, he said, "My legs are going, Mom." As the days went by he'd say, "They're almost gone." Then one day he said, "I can't feel anything below my chest." He didn't cry, didn't get angry. Just matter of fact! He never complained. Once he said, "Look, Mom, at those legs, just lying there. Useless. Isn't that something?" He was afraid he would lose the use of his arms. He'd make a fist often and move them around. I'd ask him if he hurt. He'd say, "Just checking to see if they work. That's all I need. .."'

. . . It's been raining today. It reminds me of how Steve loved the sound of rain and cloudy days made him comfortable. He also loved the sound of the leaves rustling in the wind. He said it reminded him of when he was a kid and would lie in his bed at night and listen to those big cottonwoods behind the house. .

Steve was completely paralyzed from the chest down by the time I saw him again over the Fourth of July weekend in the summer of 2000. A hospital bed had been moved into the living room of his Davenport home, and an oxygen machine droned on incessantly from a corner. Catherine and Patrick had driven up with me, and most of the rest of our family had also assembled in Davenport. Timmy, Tyler, and their cousins played raucous, nonstop games of roller hockey in the basement, vying for a Stanley Cup that Timmy had fashioned from tin-foil. We took turns bringing Steve his coffee, which he now drank through a straw, and regular servings of strawberries covered in whipped cream. One of us was always by his bed, talking to him. Strangely, there was much laughter in the chaotic house that weekend.

But shortly after we had arrived, I was walking through Steve's garage and saw his golf clubs, sitting in a corner with his golf shoes stacked on top, and all of his abandoned hockey sticks. Waves of bitterness and despair swept over me when I realized my brother, this strong, vital, athletic man who was only forty-one years old, would never again have use of such things. I found my wife on the deck out back and collapsed into sobs on her shoulder, weeping without restraint as Catherine held me, and the snot poured out of my nose and onto the deck for what seemed like an hour.

A short time later, I happened across my mom and dad in a hallway inside. I told them how bad I had felt, how angry and sad, how much I needed to purge my emotions and how much better I felt when I did. Then my dad suddenly buckled, collapsing against the wall. For months he had stood helplessly by, watching the life drain out of his son, choking back his anguish, but he could no more.

"That's what I need, too," Dad said as he began to sob.

Mom and I led him into a bedroom and rubbed his back, held him, and talked to him, while he cried. I told him how much I loved him and how it was okay to be vulnerable and feel so very sad. To think that for years I had struggled to understand my father, a journey that was often painful, and this is where it had ultimately led: to a cramped bedroom in Davenport, where, when this humble, sensitive man finally gave in to his own heartbreak, I was there to sit next to him, speaking softly, rubbing his back.

My mother was praying in the basement one morning that weekend when the telephone rang. When she answered, she heard that soft, wonderful voice at the other end of the line.

"Is this Mrs. Madigan?" the voice said.

"Why, yes, it is."

"This is Fred Rogers, calling from Pittsburgh."

"Oh, my goodness," my mother stuttered.

"I'm so very glad to meet you," Fred said.

My mother stuttered again.

"It's such a pleasure to meet you, Mister Rogers," she said. "Thanks so much for your call. Would you like to talk to Steve?"

"Yes, I would, but only if he's able."

Mom dashed the wireless receiver upstairs and handed it to Steve in his bed. "It's Mister Rogers!" she whispered.

For the next half hour, the rest of us crowded into the adjoining kitchen trying to eavesdrop on their conversation. We listened as Steve told Fred of the things he had learned in his affliction, how he still saw his disease as a blessing that had brought his family so much closer together, brought him so much closer to God, and taught him the true meaning of life. That's why I'm convinced there was human greatness on each end of the telephone line that day.

"Steve, I really hope we get to meet in person some day," Fred said.

"Yes, Fred, I do too," Steve replied. "But it looks like that will have to be in heaven."

Before they hung up, Fred asked my brother to pray for him.

Around 4:00 AM on the morning we were returning to Texas, I woke up and stumbled toward the bathroom. On the way I saw my brother grinning at me through the darkness from his hospital bed at the far end of the living room. He waved.

"What are you doing awake?" I said.

"Just laying here. What else?" Steve said. "Come have some coffee."

I laughed.

"I guess my sleep is over for the night," I said. "Could I pee first?"

"Go ahead," Steve said. "I'm not going anywhere."

I made a fresh pot and brought him a cup of strong black coffee, which he drank through a straw. He sighed with delight when he had his first sip, as he did every morning. "God, that's good," he said.

I sat in a chair beside his bed, and we talked about how much fun our kids had had together that weekend. I asked him if he was afraid, and he said just once in awhile. Steve told me what a thrill it had been for him to speak to Fred. I said that where great humans were concerned, Mister Rogers had nothing on Steve. We talked about the times we shared as boys, about all those nights in our room talking until we could talk no longer. Outside, the blackest Iowa night gradually surrendered to the first gray of dawn. We paused to listen to the breath-taking song of a cardinal who had begun to sing just outside his window. The house was quiet, except for our dusky voices. For those priceless moments we were two boys again, heart to heart, sharing the night.

A few hours later, I bent over Steve's bed and kissed him good-bye, telling him I would see him again in a few weeks.

"Life is good. So good," I wrote in my journal that day. "But how can I say that?"

Chapter 12

I was in touch with Fred at least once a week, usually more often, as my brother's condition deteriorated. "Had two conversations with Fred the last two days," I wrote in my journal in early July. "This is like walking through this stuff with Jesus himself."

In a July 8 e-mail, I told Fred that doctors had no more treatment for Steve, and that he was beginning to have difficulty breathing. On a particularly bad day of my own, I told Fred that I could not escape the horrible visions of that long, once-strong body lying in a casket, alone, deep in the ground. I spoke of my anger at the thought that the boy with whom I had spent so much of my life was coming to the premature end of his.

"You know, Fred," I said to him one day on the telephone, "if this is where a good life leads, I wonder why we bother to be good."

"I can understand how you might feel that way sometimes," Fred said.

I also mentioned to Fred the fund-raiser my siblings were hosting in the Twin Cities to help Steve and his family with their expenses. A few days later, on Tuesday, July 12, a package from Pittsburgh arrived at the St. Paul home of my sister, Terri, where the event was to take place. Inside was a Neighborhood Trolley and two copies of Fred's book, *You Are Special: Neighborly Wisdom from Mister Rogers*—one for auction at the benefit; the other "For Steve himself," as Fred wrote on a Post-it note he had attached to the cover. An envelope was also tucked into the package. When Terri opened it, she stared for several seconds, incredulous. Then she called me.

"Tim. Fred Rogers sent a check for $ 1,000," Terri said.

All that week, cards, letters, and donations continued to pour in from Steve's friends around the world. The plan had been to surprise him with the proceeds after the fund-raiser had taken place, but Steve's mounting anguish changed that.

"Steve was having a really bad day yesterday," I wrote in my journal on Wednesday, July 13. "So afraid. So discouraged. Told Mom that his mind was 'in the depths of hell.' Then she made the decision to tell him about the fund-raiser and about what Fred did, and Steve just began to sob and sob and sob.

He was completely overwhelmed, not only by Fred's gift, but by the gifts and concern of people everywhere. As I was telling [a friend] last night, all Steve's life he's felt a little 'less than', or maybe a lot 'less than.' I'm so glad that he gets to know at the end of his life how much he's loved, how much he and his life have meant to so many people."

That same week, at a restaurant in Pittsburgh, Fred sat down to dinner with another close friend of his, a successful St. Paul businessman named Phillip Bifulk. He and Fred had known each other for several years by then, having met at a weekend retreat at the Toronto community for the mentally handicapped where Henri Nouwen was the pastor. The two of them had discovered a deep spiritual kinship almost immediately, and Phillip had subsequently accepted Fred's invitation to join the board of directors of Family Communications, Inc. In fact, it was an FCI board meeting that had brought Phillip from Minnesota to Pittsburgh that week in the summer of 2000.

That night in the restaurant, Fred and Phillip talked as they typically did—about their beloved mutual friend, Nouwen; about life, death, suffering, love, grace, and the power of the Holy Spirit. In that context, Fred began to speak of a brave young man dying of cancer in Iowa, and about his large family that was rallying around him in the transition. In fact, Fred told Phillip, the man's siblings were holding a fund-raiser just that weekend in St. Paul.

"I could tell by the way he was speaking that Fred felt a very strong emotional connection to this young man and his situation," Phillip told me years later. "He felt a very strong connection to the compassion and caring of his family."

So that night in the restaurant, Phillip had an idea.

"Fred, I live there. Why don't I pay a visit to their fundraiser?" Phillip said. "That way you could be there in spirit."

"Oh, Phillip," Fred replied. "I would never ask you to do that. You don't even know these people."

"Of course I do," Phillip said. "They're children of God."

Which explained the luxury car that pulled up in front of Terri's home in St. Paul on that Saturday morning and the kindly visitor who introduced himself as Fred's friend. During the visit in her home, Phillip met my siblings and some of their friends, and said how much Fred had wanted to attend himself. Before he left, Phillip handed my sister his own check for $500, leaving Terri speechless once again.

When I tracked him down years later, I told Phillip he will always be remembered by my family as something of a mystery man, the angel who appeared that day as if from the ether, and disappeared just as quickly.

Phillip chuckled.

"I met a lot of nice people that day," he said. "I'm sure I got much more out of that visit than they did."

Later on that Saturday, dozens of others gathered in Terri's backyard, which was decorated with balloons. Her husband, Jay, displayed a wide array of items that had been collected for auction, holding up several pieces of sports paraphernalia. Then he raised the Neighborhood Trolley and an autographed book from Fred.

A few days later, Jay scanned Steve's Davenport living room with the lens of his camcorder, catching my mother as she sat on the sofa holding Terri and Jay's first child, the sleeping infant named Aedan. My dad sat at the foot of Steve's hospital bed. Cally was in a chair next to Steve, holding her husband's hand and rubbing his arm while Tyler danced around the room, mugging for the camera. Steve himself looked tired, and his pallor was a sickly gray. His mustache was gone and his brown hair had thinned. White bed sheets were pulled midway up his bare chest, and his now-lifeless feet poked out from beneath the covers at the bottom of the bed, dangling outward at sharp angles. The oxygen machine filled the room with grating noise.

"Do I look okay?" Steve said.

"You look great, Steve," my mom said. "Your hair is all fluffy."

"Okay, you can come out now," Jay said.

Steve and I were both in high school when Terri was born. But by that day she was a lovely young woman in her mid-twenties who had inherited her mother's indomitable good nature. Jay panned toward her as she emerged from a bedroom carrying a bundle of cards, letters, cash, and the checks of Fred and Phillip that Terri had wrapped in a ribbon. She set the bundle down on Steve's bare chest.

"And this isn't it," she said. "Things are still coming in . . . from every corner of the United States."

Steve's face crinkled with emotion, and he raised a hand to cover his eyes as he began to cry. Terri leaned in to kiss Steve, then hugged and kissed Cally.

"This is a happy thing," Terri said. "There's a lot of stuff there. Right now . . . there is about $10,000. We made three [thousand dollars] alone on Saturday . . . And when you read these notes, Steve. There's going to be more and more and more. Everybody says [something about] prayer in there, though they all say it in different ways . . . This is a 'thumbs-upper.'"

Steve tugged at his hair, looking at the cards and the stack of twenty- and fifty-dollar bills lying on his chest.

"'This whole two years has been a 'thumbs-upper,'" he said finally. "This is the inspiration I need to get me over the hump and get me where I want to go."

Then Terri handed Steve *You Are Special,* the book with Fred's familiar handwriting on a Post-it note on the cover. Steve opened the book to the first few pages and read the inscription.

"Thank you for your prayers," Fred had written.

Steve smiled and rubbed his eyes.

Tim Madigan

"Freddy boy," he said.

"He's calling him Fred, now," Terri said, laughing. "He knows him on a personal level."

Jay zoomed in on Steve, who looked directly into the camera.

"I just want the folks back home to know I won't let you down," Steve said, and he again began to cry.

"You've never let us down, Steve," my mother said softly.

Steve tugged at his hair some more, trying to compose himself, then looked back into the camera.

"The good Lord has a plan for us all," he said. "I have accepted my challenge. I wouldn't give it back. Nobody can have it. It's mine, and God knows I'm up for it."

"And so are we," Terri said. "This is what we can do. That's the least we can do. The prayers are most important."

Steve nodded.

"We're on a ship going one way, and sometimes it gets a little rough," he says. "But we're all in it together, by God."

"Arm-in-arm," Terri said.

Steve sniffled.

"I didn't know the meaning of arm-in-arm before," he said. "I certainly do now. Again, for the people back home, I love you all. I'm not going anywhere. Particularly when we put our arms together—for all of us—not just me. There's Dad to take care of over there."

Steve smiled and winked at my dad.

"We've got Jay to take care of," he said. "And Aedan."

Steve looked over at the month-old baby asleep in my mother's arms.

"So we're all in this together," Steve said. "Let's just teach. If we don't teach, all this crap has been for naught. We can't waste this, because this sucks. It bites the big one. But if we all learn how to teach a little better..."

". . . And love a little stronger," Terri said.

"By God, every minute of it is worth it; every second of it," Steve said. "But if we don't, then it will go for naught, and we can't let that happen. Does everybody agree?"

"We agree," my mother said. "We're teaching. We're learning."

Chapter 13

Catherine, Patrick, and I drove off from Texas before dawn on that Friday morning, July 28, and it was after 10:00 PM when we finally pulled up in front of Steve's home, where the rest of my family had already gathered. Though none of us spoke of it, we knew my brother probably had only a few more weeks to live, and thus viewed that weekend as the last chance for all of us—Steve's family, my parents and siblings, and their families—to be together while he was still alive. But when we arrived in Iowa we learned that the end was even more imminent than we had feared. My mother and sisters were waiting on Steve's front porch that night, saying they were greatly relieved to see us because his condition had deteriorated in just the last few hours.

"He's fading," my sister Chris told me on the front porch that night. "We didn't know if he would make it until you got here."

Steve seemed in a coma when I stepped into the living room, where several other relatives were quietly seated in chairs and on the sofa. I knelt by his bed, took my brother's hand in both of mine, kissed it, and began to cry. Then I heard his voice, raspy but strong.

"What's the matter?" Steve said, smiling down at me, his eyes suddenly open. "Buck up!"

Greatly startled, I stood and brushed away my tears, somewhat embarrassed as the rest of my family, as surprised as I was, began to laugh.

"I thought you were . . .," I said, not finishing the sentence.

A few minutes later, Steve called my brother Kelly to his bedside and began to tell the story of the time he had been golfing with Tiger Woods until Tiger had to drop out on the seventeenth hole because of a blister.

"I was beating him, too," Steve said.

Several of us exchanged sorrowful glances, thinking that the morphine had finally induced delirium. Then Steve winked, and the laughter started again.

"Kelly," said my brother Pat. "He's just pulling your chain."

Steve's four brothers sat up with him most of that first night, keeping vigil as he seemed to fade again in the darkness. The oxygen machine whirred in the corner as we fought off sleep, watching highlights from major league baseball games that played over and over again on the same loop of ESPN's Sports Center. When Steve stirred, I told him how much I loved him, that I had loved him longer than I'd loved anyone else.

"I love you, too," he said that night. "You look worried. Are you worried about me?"

"Yes," I said. "I'm worried about you."

"Don't be," he said. "I've got a great supporting cast."

The next morning, Steve told my mother he was ready to "close this chapter."

"Do you think so, Steve?" my mother asked.

"Yes," he said.

"Are you at peace?" my mother asked.

"Yes," he said. "I want to have a team meeting. Call the troops."

About thirty of us filed into the living room, and at Steve's command we joined hands. But rather than closing a chapter, he seemed more determined than ever to fight on. It was as if he had drawn strength and hope from the morning sunlight that poured into the room from the window behind his head. Someone shut off the oxygen machine so we could hear him.

"I've been looking around at the faces and I see fear and that's understandable," he said. "I see anxiety. That's understandable. But there's still a lot of fight in me . . . I've carried this stuff inside of me for a long time now. I can't carry it by myself anymore. I need each of you to take a chunk of it and smash it."

He paused, cleared his throat, and pointed toward little Aedan, who was being held by his mother.

"New life," he said.

He paused again, tugging at his hair.

"I hope I will be here in ten years," he said. "My odds are probably the worst of anybody in this room, but my odds weren't very good when I started this . . . We've all grown as a family through this. Now we can help other families. We can help other families raise their children . . . Never assume there is going to be more than this day. We must never take love for granted."

Steve looked around the room at each of us.

"There's [all these people] inside this room and a gazillion people outside of this room who need love," he said. "So when you go to sleep tonight, thank God for tomorrow. Life isn't about what you've done, but what you can do."

He paused again, and cleared his throat.

"I love you all," Steve said. "Thank you for getting me this far."

He smiled, and we crowded around his bed, piling our hands on top of his, and letting out a cheer that echoed out the front door and down the quiet street.

A few hours later, a shy, gray-haired priest named Randy arrived at the front door, and we crowded into the living room for the second time that day, holding hands and weeping while saying the Lord's Prayer. At Steve's request, the priest read the framed passage of *Living Faith*, then administered the Catholic rites for the sick. He placed a wafer of communion on Steve's tongue, calling it "food for the journey."

The priest came again the following day, but this time, for some reason, there were no tears as we joined hands to pray. Steve also had deemed that day, a Sunday, "picture day," so we crowded around his bed in two dozen different combinations and smiled for the camera.

"How do I look?" Steve asked between each shot.

If he blinked or felt his smile wasn't just right, Steve insisted that the photo be snapped again.

"Not good enough," Steve would order. "Reshoot!"

That night, Dad, my three youngest brothers, and I went out to a nearby Irish pub, ordering glasses of draft beer for ourselves, and an extra one that we sat in the middle of the table. When we had finished our own beers that night, we took turns sipping the one that had been poured for Steve.

It was my brother Pat who began to sob in the pub that night, overcome by the terrible sadness that we all felt. But back at Steve's home, we found a party, not a wake. Steve had decided to create his own version of the game of Clue, assigning each of us wacky aliases and crimes that we were alleged to have committed. Most details of the game escape me now, but I remember that Steve dubbed his son Timmy, "Wink Dinkerman." He also charged my brother Mike with the crime of having poor taste in girlfriends. To hear the riotous laughter that came from the living room that night, no one passing by could have guessed that a death vigil was taking place inside the house. Steve entertained us for hours. Something supernatural lived in him that night, a gigantic gust of his great spirit that would help sustain us all in the days ahead.

For by Monday morning, it was clear that Steve was preparing to die. He slept more and more often, and when he was awake, found it increasingly difficult to breathe. On Tuesday, the hospice nurse said one of Steve's lungs had collapsed and that she didn't expect him to live until the weekend. I was sitting at the far end of the living room that Tuesday afternoon when Steve called Timmy and Tyler to his bedside and told his sons that he probably had only a day or two more to live.

It was around dinnertime that day when Steve said he wanted to have a beer, which he drank through a straw as we raised our own glasses to him and sang "For He's a Jolly Good Fellow."

But there would be no more games of Clue that night, no more hours of riotous laughter. The final passage had begun.

About midnight on that Tuesday, I was sitting by Steve's bed when my mother came to say good night, a moment that will be seared on my heart for as long as I live. My brother was sleeping then, so I watched as she held his hand and slowly rubbed his long arm that poked out from beneath the bed sheet. My mother kissed Steve gently on his forehead, his cheek, and his forehead again as she quietly wept.

"I love you, Steve," she said softly. "I love you, Steve."

Then she rubbed his arm one last time and forced herself to shuffle off to her bed. So much of Steve's illness recalled for me the New Testament stories I had been taught in Catholic school about the passion and death of Jesus. That night by Steve's bed, I had the powerful sense that my mother was just like Mary, the Mother of Christ, keeping her heartbreaking vigil at the foot of the Cross.

While awake, Steve continued to greet each person who came into his room, flashing a brief smile and struggling to give visitors a "thumbs up." On Tuesday, my sister Terri placed young Aedan on Steve's chest, and my brother gently kissed the top of the infant's head and stroked his face. Older nieces and nephews stopped by his bed to keep vigil in between games of roller hockey or playing out back.

"Is your sickness better, Uncle Steve?" asked Riley, a five-year-old niece.

On Wednesday, Steve woke up briefly to greet a relative named Paula who had driven in that day from Chicago.

"Beautiful," he said to her when Paula took his hand. "Do I look okay?"

Well after midnight on Thursday, Steve woke up again and smiled when my brother-in-law, Jay, arrived from Minneapolis.

But Steve's breathing became more difficult with every passing hour, and panic would often cross his face when he was awake and struggled for air, so we tried to keep him sedated.

That Thursday morning, I woke up at 6:30 AM to take my shift at his bedside, sitting in the living room with Jay and my brother Mike. At 7:50 that morning, Jay and I were talking about fishing when I saw Steve stir, open his eyes, and rise up out of his bed, lifting both arms toward the ceiling like he had just scored a goal in hockey. Then Steve slumped back down, and by the time I got to his bed, my brother's breathing had changed dramatically, becoming shallower and shallower. Within seconds, each member of our family had surrounded the bed. Cally wept at Steve's side. Timmy and Tyler looked frightened and confused at the foot of the bed. My mother held a rosary, praying and crying. My father's face crinkled with emotion. I held Steve's left hand and rubbed his forehead, and told him to go be with the angels. Then his breathing stopped.

For nearly two years, ever since Steve was diagnosed, I had thought about that moment, wondering what it would be like. But nothing could have prepared me for what I felt as my brother died that morning. In an instant, it seemed as if all the oxygen had been sucked out of the room, replaced by an absence more profound than any I had felt before. The same long body was still lying in the hospital bed, but the unseen thing that had made my brother who he was had gone, had vanished in a mysterious instant. What was that invisible presence that had been the essence of my brother? Where did it go on that sunny August morning? Where is it now? They are questions I will ask as long as I am alive myself.

Someone finally shut off the oxygen machine, and there was an eerie stillness in the house. The family lingered by Steve's body for many minutes, kissing him and saying good-bye, then most left the living room and sat together weeping in the bright sunshine of the back porch. My father and I stayed behind in the living room as funeral home attendants loaded my brother's body into a black bag. Dad and I walked next to the gurney as the attendants carried Steve's body to the white van parked in the driveway. Then we joined the others out back.

"My heart's broke," I told my mother.

"I know," she said.

For the first time that morning, I began to sob.

My first telephone call was to my wife, who had returned to Texas with Patrick the day before. My second was to the office of Fred Rogers.

"Oh, Tim," he said. "I'm so sorry. I had no idea it was coming so soon."

I have no real clue how we spent the rest of that day, probably moving about in a shocked and grieving stupor. I do know that it was on the night of Steve's death that Fred's e-mail message arrived in Steve's computer, was printed, and passed from hand to hand inside my brother's house. The subject line read: "Dear Tim."

After a long day at work I came home and told Joanne about Steve. We talked about you all during dinner. Joanne sends her love to you, too. As usual I went for my after-dinner walk in the park near our apartment. It was near sunset. . . and a gorgeous one it was. On my way back there was the most beautiful cloud formation illuminated by the last bit of setting sun. Tim, there are no adequate words for such beauty. At any rate all I could think of saying was "Thank You," so I did, and I prayed for you and your wonderful family gathered in such common purpose there in Iowa. It wasn't long before something said to me, "Look up." Well, I did and there in a completely clear patch of sky was the brightest new moon I had ever seen. It looked a special apostrophe in the sky, and I thought, "Yep, it's Steve's for sure."

Just wanted you to know that you're all in our hearts. . . more than ever.

IPOY, as always. Fred

Chapter 14

But even then the world did not stop. (I remember checking the baseball box scores the morning after Steve died.) Over the next few days, we helped Cally go about the surreal tasks of selecting a casket and a cemetery plot. As a family we relived, moment by moment, the sacred times we had spent with Steve in the days before he died. Timmy and Tyler continued to rollerblade with their cousins. My three surviving brothers and I went to a shopping mall to purchase a suit for Steve to be buried in.

"How does it wear underground?" Pat asked a horrified clerk at a clothing store as the rest of us bent over laughing.

We settled on an expensive suit of navy blue and a silk tie. Friends and family arrived from around the nation to pay their respects to my brother, whose body lay in an open casket in a large room of a Davenport funeral home. When I kissed the forehead of Steve's body it was cold and hard as stone. I could see my nine-year-old son Patrick trying to make sense of things, wondering how Uncle Steve could be talking and laughing one day, and in that casket the next. Yet at times, the days before the funeral had the feel of a typical family reunion, and as I saw people I hadn't seen in years, I was surprised by how comforted I was to see my oldest friends and favorite relatives.

But there was no laughter, no small talk on the Monday morning after Steve died, as the family gathered at the funeral home to say good-bye one last time. I knelt by my brother's body a few minutes before they closed his casket, studying his hands and his face, studying the same body that had joined me in all those boyhood games, the flesh and blood that had lain below me in the bottom bunk as the cottonwood leaves shimmered just outside our bedroom window, the same body that had inspired and entertained us just a few days before.

The word sorrow does not do justice to the feelings that swept over me then. They sprang forth from a place deepest within me, overwhelming me with an intensity I had never experienced before. After the first sob the others poured forth without restraint as I said Steve's name, over and over. But even in my anguish I was aware that I was not alone. I heard the soft sound of my wife's voice, consoling me from behind. And as I wept I felt two hands gently come to rest on my shoulders. When I glanced sideways, I recognized the strong hands of my father.

The full significance of that moment did not dawn on me until a few days later, but when it did, I realized that a circle of life had closed. I had hungered for my father's comfort as a child, looking to him as I lay in the dirt. But then, by my brother's body, in the moment of my greatest devastation, my father had put aside his own grief to love and support me, standing with his hands on my trembling shoulders. I came to realize that in so many important ways, they had been there all along.

The Davenport Catholic church was crowded for the funeral. After communion, Steve's siblings joined hands near the pulpit as I read the brief eulogies that each of my brothers and sisters had written the night before. They wrote of his courage, his faith, his sense of humor, his love for his family, and his desperate desire to see the Minnesota Vikings win a Super Bowl. I spoke of my own memories of the tender boy in the bottom bunk, and the sound of the cottonwood leaves outside our bedroom window back home in Minnesota. I managed to remain composed as I looked down from the pulpit that day, even as I saw the weeping young boys in the front pew, Steve's former players, all of them dressed in their white hockey jerseys.

The funeral procession stretched for miles, leading to the top of a green hill in a beautiful cemetery. The priest said prayers at the gravesite, and we laid red roses on Steve's casket before returning to the limousines for the ride home.

Back at Steve's place, we sat around the kitchen table, quietly talking about the day. Not five minutes after we sat down, a Federal Express truck pulled up out front and a deliveryman knocked at the front door, holding a package from Pittsburgh that was addressed to Tim Madigan. I could tell by the handwriting that it had come from Fred, but under the circumstances, I assumed that the package was meant for my nephew, Steve's son, Timmy.

So it was the boy who opened it, sitting across the table from me. Inside the package he found two large, identical black-and-white photographs of a pair of cute little boys, each picture framed in expensive brown wood. There was a moment of uncertainty then, because no one on Timmy's side of the table recognized the boys in the photograph. It was surely kind of him to think of the family, but why would Mister Rogers send framed photographs of two boys who were strangers? I, too, thought that was somewhat odd.

"Here," I said. "Let me see."

My heart lurched toward my throat when I first saw the photographs. They were in black and white—two little boys, their skin fluorescent in the summer sun, bellies sticking out over their shorts, boys who were nearly conjoined in some way, a package deal in a small-town Minnesota boyhood. The framed photographs were copies of the same cherished snapshot I had sent Fred a few weeks earlier. He had indeed returned them special delivery.

"Dear Tim. Our love is with you and all the Madigan Family," Fred wrote in the note he had enclosed. "Life after life will always be a mystery until we have the 'eyes to see' what Steve now sees. Grace and peace to the best brother ever. IPOY. Fred."

I looked across the table at Timmy and smiled.

"Those aren't just any two boys," I said. "That's your dad and me. Mister Rogers sent us pictures of your dad and me when we were little."

On the day he buried his father, Timmy grinned broadly.

Chapter 15

My two greatest mentors in the essential art of grieving were, remarkably enough, the children's television legend, Mister Rogers, and a child who grew up watching his program, my young son, Patrick. Together, they helped liberate me from a soul-killing stoicism that had imprisoned me for most of my life.

Fred's teachings along those lines began the day I met him, as he shared his own difficult feelings about the loss of his friend, Jim Stumbaugh, and talked about pounding extra hard on the keys of his piano as a means of expressing his own grief.

"With grief there is, inevitably, some times of anger and you know, God can take our anger," he had told me that first day in his office. "I think God respects the fact that we would share a whole gamut of feelings."

Then came that unforgettable morning in 1996, when Henri Nouwen died and Fred called to share himself with me at his most vulnerable; and all the other times over the years when Fred's wisdom and non-judging heart coaxed my own anguish out into the open.

Patrick's teaching came indirectly, but was no less profound. The story of how that occurred was something that Fred and I had talked about often over the years, one that began on a December afternoon in 1996, when I was still greatly afflicted by the Furies. That day, our family had just piled into our minivan to run a short errand, when this question came from a small voice in the backseat:

"Dad," said Patrick, who was five years old then, "how come I've never seen you cry?"

What could possibly have inspired such a question, I have no idea. There was no warning or preamble. One minute it was, "Mom, what's for supper?" and the next it was, "Dad, how come ..."

Catherine was seated next to me in the front seat that day and as surprised by the question as me. But my wife has always been one of those fortunate souls for whom tears came naturally, were spilled spontaneously, and were quickly forgotten. Patrick had seen his mother cry dozens of times by then. So my wife was entitled to turn to me with a wry smile on her face that said, "Answer this one, Dad."

I couldn't, of course, mumbling something then about crying when Patrick was not around, at sad movies and so forth. But, as I told Fred during one of my visits to Pittsburgh, I knew immediately that my young son had put his finger on an inability that, as much as anything, had kept me wedded to my own torment. Simply put, I could not cry. Like so many men, I swallowed my rage, my sadness, even my joy—calm and seemingly stalwart on the outside while the Furies secretly raged within.

I could only hope that the same debilitating handicap would not be passed on to my son. Hence my conversation with Patrick on another sunny December afternoon just the day after his surprising question. He and I were back in the van after playing at a park near our home. Before pulling out, I turned to my son and thanked him for his curiosity. Tears were a very good thing for both boys and girls, I said. Crying is God's way of healing people when they are sad.

"I'm very glad you can cry whenever you're sad or whenever you're angry," I said. "Sometimes daddies have a harder time showing how they feel. You know, Patrick, I wish I were more like you in that way. Someday I hope I can do better."

Patrick nodded, as if he understood, but I held out little hope for myself. Until then, I could count on one hand the number of times I had openly wept (one of them being the day I received Fred's first IPOY letter just a few months earlier). A lifetime of sadness and anger was buried inside me, but old habits were hard to break. I figured it would take something on the order of a miracle for me to connect with the dusty core of my own emotions in any real way. After Patrick's question just before Christmas that year, I prayed that I could somehow be restored to just a few of my own unshed tears.

From the time he was an infant, Patrick had enjoyed an unusual passion and affinity for music. By age four, he could pound out several bars of Wagner's "The Ride of the Valkyries" by ear on the piano. He spent hours as a child singing along with the sound track to *The Hunchback of Notre Dame*, and conducting the orchestral pieces. But these were hidden pleasures for him, enjoyed in the privacy of his own room or with the small and forgiving audience of his mother, father, and older sister, Melanie. What the youth director of our church was suggesting that same holiday season was something different altogether. She called to ask if Patrick would sing a verse of "Away in a Manger" during the Christmas Eve service.

"You know, Mom," Patrick said when he found out, "sometimes when I have to do something important, I get kind of scared."

Yet he decided to move forward with his debut, and for the next week diligently practiced his part. I was told a rehearsal at the church had gone exceedingly well. But I could only envision myself at age five, singing into a microphone before hundreds of people. When Christmas Eve arrived, my expectations for Patrick's performance were modest indeed.

My palms were damp by the time of his solo, which came late in the service. Then, in the darkened sanctuary, a spotlight found my young son as he stood alone at the microphone, dressed in white and in angel's wings. And he sang as if he had done so forever. Patrick hit every note, slowly, confidently, and for those few moments he seemed transformed. There was eternity in my son's voice that night, a penetrating beauty rich enough to dissolve centuries of manly reserve. At the sound of Patrick's voice, tears built at the corners of my eyes and spilled down my cheeks.

His song was soon over, and as the congregation applauded, my wife and daughter brushed away their own tears. After the service, I moved quickly to congratulate Patrick, but found he had other priorities.

"Mom," he said, "I really have to go to the bathroom."

But I knew I had only a short window before the stoicism closed back around my heart. I was waiting for my son when he came out of the restroom.

"Patrick, I need to talk to you about something," I said, sniffling.

Alarm crossed his face.

"Is it something bad?" he asked.

"No, it's not something bad," I answered.

"Is it something good?"

"It's very good."

I took him by the hand and led him down a long hallway, into a darkened room where we could be alone. I knelt to his height and admired his young face in the shadows, the large blue eyes, the dusting of freckles on his nose and cheeks, the dimple on one side. He looked at my moist eyes quizzically, with concern.

"Patrick, do you remember when you asked me why you had never seen me cry?" I began.

He nodded.

"Well, I'm crying now, aren't I?" I said, and he nodded again.

"Why are you crying, Dad?" he asked.

"Your singing was so pretty, it made me cry."

Patrick smiled proudly and flew into my arms. I began to sob.

"Sometimes," my five-year-old son said into my shoulder that night, "life is so beautiful, you just have to cry."

That was the night I became a fountain, relatively speaking. After years of stuffing my anger, rage, sadness, and pretty much everything else into the dark vault of my depression, feelings regularly began pouring out of me in waves, generally in the privacy of my car as I listened to sad music. Each time they did, I felt lighter, more alive, more connected to the world around me. The murky reservoir of the Furies began to recede.

And I thank God that by the time Steve got sick, I was able to cry. I wept on the long drives back and forth from Davenport and on his deck out back, and at his casket on that tragic Monday morning. Back home in Texas after his funeral, I often disappeared onto the small roads that traverse the rolling countryside near Fort Worth, clinging to the memories of our shared boyhood, trying to preserve them second by second as the tears poured down my face. One song by Celine Dion, the theme from the movie Titanic, was sure to induce a gusher. The songs of folk-rock artist Dan Fogelberg were favorite grieving music, too, particularly his lullaby-like duet with Emmylou Harris called "Only the Heart May Know." I found the song so affecting that, a few weeks after Steve's death, I typed out a few lines of the lyrics and e-mailed them to Fred.

Silent sea, tell this to me:
Where are the children
that we used to be?

I remember that Fred replied almost immediately from The Crooked House on Nantucket.

"Oh, Tim, this is so beautiful," he wrote. "I'm looking out at a very silent sea right now and thinking of you . . . and answering the question of the song by saying:

'The children that we used to be are right within us and will always be. Your childhood with Steve can never be taken away from you. You'll take it with you to heaven, just as he has already done. Imagine the 'advocates' that we have on the Other Side!! All those who are ready to welcome us with open arms ('wings'!!).

"Your grief lived and observed is another of Steve's gifts to you," Fred wrote. 'Those gifts, whatever they may be, will never die."

Every four years, thirty of the world's finest young pianists congregate in Fort Worth for the Van Cliburn International Piano Competition, a kind of cultural Olympics that attracts worldwide attention. Because of his love for the instrument and his friendship with Van, I encouraged Fred to attend the latest competition, which was to begin in the spring of 2001. For various reasons, Fred could not make the trip, yet, as it turned out, the Cliburn competition helped bring us together again.

I learned that one of the 2001 competitors was a young woman who studied at the Cleveland Institute of Music, and I quickly volunteered to fly north to interview her for the *Star-Telegram*. As I made my travel plans, I made certain there would be plenty of time for the short drive east to Pittsburgh.

Just before leaving for Cleveland, I sent Fred my essay that had been published in the *Star-Telegram* a few weeks earlier, on May 2, 2001. The piece had been inspired, strangely enough, by the soft drink called Mountain Dew.

"In the beginning," the essay began, "I was a brown-pop kid."

On summer mornings in Minnesota, my brother Steve and I rode bikes across town to Little League games, and on our way home, stopped at the lumberyard owned by my dad. Inside the office, Dad kept a pop machine that for a dime dispensed ice-cold bottles of Coca-Cola, which tasted very good.

I didn't learn of the alternate universe of Mountain Dew drinkers until I was thirteen or so. That was when friends introduced my brother and me to

145

Chet's Place, which was a combination of adolescent fraternity, clubhouse and machine shop, where all of the guys drank Dew, and where, over the next several years, some of the sweetest, most innocent hours of my boyhood were spent.

Why should I remember Chet's now? For years as an adult, I've enjoyed Mountain Dew with my sandwiches at lunch. Yet it was only recently, sitting at my desk, happily sipping a Dew, munching on a mouthful of crushed ice, that I realized my current preference in sodas might be due to more than just its pleasing taste.

The soft drink story really begins on a very sad day in 1958 when a boy named Tommy Dahlgren died of cancer on his eighth birthday. Chet was his father, a strapping World War II veteran with a buzz top haircut, and at the time a member of the police force in Crookston. After his only child died, Chet could no longer stomach the inevitable police calls to fatal accidents, so he quit the force and set up a machine shop behind his house. He also stocked not one but two pop machines in his shop, and he bought boxes of red licorice, Snickers bars, Salted Nut Rolls, lots of bubble gum, cheese and crackers and potato chips, hoping that neighborhood kids might come and visit his workplace, keep him company for a little while, perhaps relieve a little of the sting of his grief.

It was a small, dark and dingy place, Chet's was, crowded with machines used to sharpen saw blades. Hand tools were strewn everywhere. There was an old sofa beneath the window, alongside barber chairs Chet had found somewhere, an old card table, a large wooden spool turned on end and also used for card games, a few folding chairs, a black-and-white television on a shelf at one end of the room (where we watched President Nixon's resignation speech at Chet's one night, but almost nothing else), a huge antique radio and a fireplace where Chet burned thick logs in winter.

146

I'm Proud of You

And empty Mountain Dew bottles, green bottles like beer cups after a college frat party, empty bottles rolling around on the floor, or abandoned on the shelves, or stacked on the machines. One of Chet's two soda machines, in fact, was filled with nothing but Dew. Why brown pop was shunned at Chet's, I don't really know. Maybe it was Mountain Dew's relative novelty at the time, or that particular soda's magnificent taste. Anyway, within days of our arriving as members of Chet's gang, my brother and I were converts, our brown-pop days in the past. We hung at Chet's almost every night and drank Dew, one after another, just like the other guys.

Our parents were grateful for Chet's, because how much trouble can you get into in a machine shop? We were grateful, too, in our way. We checked our small-town adolescent worries at Chet's door, and believed that life would always be that simple.

But it couldn't, of course. My own hours at Chet's dwindled my junior year in high school, when I fell in love for the first time. There had to have been a last visit to the place, a last Mountain Dew drunk in Chet's shop, but I don't remember it. It probably came when I was visiting from college, by which time a new generation of boys had taken over the place.

It wasn't long after our years together at Chet's that the harsher realties began to intrude on our lives. One of the guys was killed in a terrible fire in the high school auto shop. Another of the regulars at Chet's took his own life by lying down in front of a train. Another guy began a struggle with alcohol that went on for many sad years.

Some of us became lawyers, or farmers or entrepreneurs, or engineers or writers. We got married and had families of our own, wishing our children had a place like Chet's, a place as simple and safe and fun, but so far as I know, none of our offspring has found it.

Last August we buried my brother Steve after his long, painful and brave fight against lung cancer. I see him now inside Chet's, a half-full bottle of Mountain Dew at his side as he sits at a card table, a thin teen-age boy tugging nervously at a mop of long brown hair while he bends over the cards in his hands. His eyes blaze with intensity as he plays. My heart soars and aches at the same time as I remember this, and I wonder again why life couldn't always be so nice.

It sounds almost ridiculous to think about it now—drinking pop, playing cards in a machine shop, hanging out—someone's sanguine fantasy of small-town youth. But it isn't. I was there, and I want to go back to Chet's if only for a night, only for an hour, hang with my brother and the guys and feel again what it's like to be young and without care. But I can't. I guess that's what memories are for, memories and the odd adult sip of Mountain Dew.

On the first night of my visit, Fred suggested an Indian restaurant near the Pitt campus. It was a dark, quiet place with spicy food. We talked about Steve for most of our meal. I told Fred about the extraordinary days of tears and laughter in Steve's house in the week before he died, how my brother had sustained and inspired us.

"We were so lucky to be with him then," I said. "Think of all the families that don't have that opportunity. We all miss Steve terribly, but if he had to die, sometimes I think his was the perfect death."

"It was a grace-filled time, for sure," Fred said, shaking his head in wonder.

I described the last moment of my brother's life, when he opened his eyes and rose up from his bed, his arms lifted toward the ceiling.

"A gesture of triumph," Fred said, smiling.

I told Fred about the profound absence I felt in Davenport the moment Steve died that morning.

We discussed the power and intensity of grief—anger and despair one day, gratitude the next, deep sadness the day after that.

"Sometimes, though, I feel like he's with me more now than ever," I told Fred that night.

"Maybe he is," Fred said. "You know, Tim, there is such a thin veil between this life and whatever comes after it."

It was when we had finished dessert, and were preparing to leave our table that a look of alarm crossed Fred's face.

"My goodness," he said. "I almost forgot. I need to get something from my car."

"Please sit down," I said. "Give me your keys. I'll get it. Just tell me what it is."

"No," Fred said. "This will just take me a second."

He rose, and I watched as he hurried from the restaurant, returning a few minutes later. When he did, he carried a large paper sack. Back at our table, he removed a twenty-four- ounce plastic bottle of Mountain Dew from the sack and, with great ceremony, sat the bottle down in front of me. Fred was beaming as he returned to his seat across the table.

"I went several places trying to find Mountain Dew in a glass bottle, but I'm afraid this is the best I could do," Fred said, still grinning.

I could not find the words to respond.

The next morning, Fred stopped by his office to retrieve what he said was a particularly helpful book on grief, which I read in the lobby of his health club while he went for his swim. We ate breakfast together and sat talking in the lobby for a long time after that. The year before, Fred had decided to stop producing the television show and he told me that morning that he was very happy with the decision. No more fiddling with those contact lenses, he said. After nine hundred episodes, it was time for him to take on other work for children, possibly something related to the Internet.

I remember that he seemed particularly languid that morning, relaxed after his swim and slumped casually on a sofa. There was an easy comfort between us, more so than ever before, a familiarity born of love, trust, and common experience. As I sat with him that morning, I remembered looking forward to dozens of such visits in the future, for I always assumed I would be an old man myself by the time Fred died. He took such good care of his body, his spirit was the healthiest of any human I knew, and the world clearly needed him more than ever. I had no inkling that when I hugged him and told him good-bye on that rainy spring morning in Pittsburgh, I would never see my friend again.

Chapter 16

When Fred was a boy in Latrobe, his mother taught him how to look for hope during the darkest times.

"In times of tragedy, look for the helpers," Nancy McFeely Rogers would often tell her son.

"'They're always there. Perhaps on the sidelines, but the helpers are always there."

Fred never forgot his mother's admonition, never stopped looking for the helpers and celebrating them, which was certainly true in the days after the terrorist attacks of September 11, 2001. While shocked and saddened by the nightmare of that day, Fred also marveled at the firefighters and police officers at the World Trade Center who died trying to save people they didn't know; and all those who tirelessly dug through the rubble in the aftermath; and the thousands who lined up to give blood. When we talked by telephone on a Thursday night nine days later, Fred told me of a young violinist from the Juilliard School who played for rescue workers until she could no longer lift her arms.

Actually, it was Catherine who spoke to Fred first when he called our home that night, telling our friend how we had tried to tide our children through the horror while nursing our own wrenching sadness. As the two of them talked, I actually remember becoming impatient for my turn on the telephone because I had thought of Fred so often since 9/11, wondering how a man of his spiritual insight and greatness would come to terms with such evil. Nancy McFeely Rogers, as it turned out, would have been proud.

"'There are always helpers," he told me that night. "'This country has demonstrated that better than I ever could have imagined."

I was struck by the peace in Fred's voice that night, a calm that reflected his deep faith in the ultimate goodness of humanity that, if anything, had deepened in the days since the attacks. I remember feeling strangely peaceful that night myself and told him so.

"As horrible as this has been, I just feel like this is a real opportunity, a turning point where people have a chance to make a real difference in the world," I said. "Does that sound strange?"

"Not at all," Fred said. "In some ways, I feel the same."

I told him that the catastrophe inspired me to try and live out the words of my favorite prayer.

"I bet you know it," I said. "It begins, 'Dear God, make me an instrument of your peace.'"

Fred immediately recognized the first line of the Prayer of St. Francis. He answered with the second.

"Where there is hatred, let me sow love," Fred said.

"Where there is injury, pardon," I said.

Then, for the rest of the prayer, Fred and I alternated, line by line, speaking quietly on the telephone.

Where there is doubt, faith;
Where there is despair, hope;
Where there is darkness, light;
Where there is sadness, joy;

O Divine Master,
Grant that I not so much seek to be consoled as to console,
To be understood as to understand,
To be loved, as to love.
For it is in giving that we receive,
It is in pardoning that we are pardoned,
And it is in dying that we are born to eternal life.

There was a long silence on the line when we finished, as Fred and I let our shared prayer make its way into the ailing universe. He was the first one to speak, and I still remember how surprised and pleased I was by what he said.

"I can't tell you how often I pray to Steve for guidance," Fred said. "I'm so grateful to you for having made that connection for me."

That night, before we hung up, I spoke briefly to Joanne and the two of us shared a laugh together. Then, with Fred back on the line, I told him again how much I loved him. "And I love you, too," he said.

They were the last spoken words we would ever exchange.

Several months later, in February 2002, Caroline Kennedy's book *The Best-Loved Poems of Jacqueline Kennedy Onassis* was a huge best seller, which was what inspired my newspaper assignment to solicit the favorite poems of other celebrities. I contacted historian David McCullough, who chose the Colonial American epic 'The Listeners," by Walter de La Mare. Singer Don Henley mentioned "Invictus," by W. E Henley; Martin Sheen, "Gitanjali," by Rabindranath Tagore; George Will, "Casey at the Bat," by

Ernest Lawrence Thayer. And I managed to persuade one other celebrity to share his favorite, though Fred did much more than identify a poem. He offered another window into his magnificent soul.

'Thanks to your recent request I've been thinking a lot about 'poems'... a LOT . . .," Fred wrote to me in an e-mail. "And mostly about poems I learned when I was a young boy and a very young man (from Chaucer through Shakespeare and Auden and Keats and Browning . . .), which in itself shows me the importance of our earliest education.

Those lines which we read, and sometimes memorize, at the beginning of our lives travel with us all our days. "This above all; to thine own self be true. And it must follow, as the night the day, Thou canst not be false to any man." And so I must admit there is a "favorite" poem from every poet I have ever loved. But to choose one favorite I find myself going even further back in my life to a psalm of King David, which my parents recited to me many, many times when I was very, very young.

"The Lord is my Shepherd, I shall not want. He maketh me to lie down in green pastures..."

I can hear both my mother's and my father's voices saying that psalm. I probably didn't know what a lot of it meant but obviously it meant a lot to them and they meant a lot to me . . . Through my life, I've studied that psalm—that song, that poem—in different English translations as well as in different languages and have read countless scholarly commentaries, and while I have long since given up the "thees" and "thous" of most biblical translations, the Psalm 23 that I repeat every day is the one my parents "taught" me all those years ago. In 1970, when my Dad was very ill and I had to go on a two-day work trip I remember as vividly as if it were only yesterday the last things we talked about. . . his beloved evergreens (Dad loved to plant and admire pine trees!) . . . and right after that we just naturally said the 23rd Psalm together. The next day, while I was away, Dad died. "I will dwell in the house of the Lord forever" are the last words we spoke with each other in this life.

I watched him on an Internet video stream, striding happily into the East Room of the White House in his snappy blue suit and obviously fresh haircut, taking a place next to that day's other honorees such as Nancy Reagan, home-run king Hank Aaron, and tenor Placido Domingo. On that Tuesday, September 9, 2002, Fred smiled broadly as President Bush hung around his neck the Presidential Medal of Freedom, the highest honor given to an American civilian.

"Fred Rogers has proven that television can soothe the soul and nurture the spirit and teach the very young," the president said that day. "The whole idea,' says the beloved host of Mister Rogers' Neighborhood, 'is to look at the television camera and present as much love as you possibly could to a person who needs it.' This message of unconditional love has won Fred Rogers a very special place in the heart of a lot of moms and dads all across America."

As I watched, sitting at home in Texas, the question came to me once again: How was it that I, of all the people in the world, had come to know, love, and be loved by this man of historic goodness? I sent Fred an e-mail message that day, congratulating him, and thanking him again for being my friend. Almost immediately I received his gracious reply, after which he again signed off, "IPOY."

Later that week, I received another message, this one from my mother, who was also thrilled by Fred's recognition.

"What an honor and so deserved," she wrote. "Please pass on our congratulations to him. You might mention to him that every time I see a quarter moon, I think of him and that beautiful e-mail he sent right after Steve died. He certainly has a special place in my heart."

I forwarded that message to Fred.

"Dear Tim," Fred replied. "Reading what you sent from your mom made me cry. Somehow I feel so 'connected' to you all. First it was you and our times together. Then it was your sharing Steve with me (through his sickness and death). And now all your spirits seem to support me wherever I may be. Gratefully, Fred.

"P.S. Your mom must be so proud of you, dear Tim. You are an extraordinary human being, and I feel blessed to be able to call you 'friend.'"

Then came another message from my mother: "Wow, Tim . . . How honored do I feel . . . We are so blessed to think that he has us in his huge circle of friends. Yes. We are very proud of you, Tim. You have blessed us in many ways, but most of all because of what you do. God bless you always. With Mister Rogers keeping us in his prayers, it doesn't get any better than that."

No, Mother, it doesn't.

Chapter 17

In my home today there are reminders of Fred Rogers almost everywhere I look. A Mister Rogers coffee mug sits by my computer as I work, the crystal starfish on a shelf just above my head. On another bookshelf down the hall is the photograph of Steve and me as young boys—one of the framed copies Fred sent to Davenport on the day of my brother's funeral. (The other is with Steve's wife and sons in Iowa.) From another bookshelf in our family room, Fred and I smile out at a camera, standing arm in arm on the set of Mister Rogers' Neighborhood in 1995. On top of my bedroom dresser resides the Mister Rogers commemorative watch he sent to me in 2001 after taping the last episode of Mister Rogers' Neighborhood.

And carefully tucked away in a filing cabinet is seven years of correspondence, a stack of letters and e-mail from Pittsburgh several inches thick. As a matter of course, I keep Fred's first IPOY letter on the very top and leaf through the stack every few months at least, growing incredulous and teary-eyed all over again.

Yet every time I do, I'm also saddened by the fact that in that stack there are just a handful of letters and electronic messages from the last year or so of Fred's life, and for that, I am to blame. We were in contact much less toward the end because I was finally happy, the Furies pretty much vanquished. I still thought of Fred nearly every day, gave thanks for his friendship, and loved him more than ever. I took great comfort in the knowledge that he was out there, waiting at the other end of a phone call, e-mail message, or flight to Pittsburgh. But quite simply I needed him less.

There was also that part of me, I admit, that had begun to take our friendship for granted, part of me that believed that he would somehow live forever—that there would be many years for more trips to Pittsburgh, that there was another thick stack of loving correspondence yet to be written. And I was wrong.

In late September 2002, I was pleasantly surprised by a postcard from St. Andrews, Scotland.

"Thinking of you in this marvelous town," Fred wrote. "Its colleges are ancient though obviously lively. This is a brief yet interesting tour of such an extra special country. Love, Fred."

About a month later, I received an e-mail from Pittsburgh with "IPOY" in the subject line, Fred's response to my weeklong newspaper series on the Jim Crow era in Fort Worth that I had mailed to him a few days before. "Masterful work," he said.

But much more pleasing to me from that note was his news that he and Joanne would be in Dallas the following January for the premiere of a symphony inspired by the songs of Mister Rogers' Neighborhood. Finally, it seemed certain that Fred would be a guest in my home, meet my family, see my Neighborhood and thus have the truest sense of my life. That visit, I thought, would make our friendship complete.

But in mid-December, I learned through a press release that unspecified personal reasons would prevent Fred from attending the symphony premiere. I immediately sent him an e-mail, expressing my disappointment and concern for him and his family. For the first time in our seven-year friendship, I never heard back.

The week before Christmas, I sent him a small pamphlet on Benedictine spirituality that I had come to cherish, *Always We Begin Again,* and was greatly relieved to receive a note from Fred in reply. It was dated the day after Christmas, and written in his same distinctive hand.

"Oh, Tim . . . Thank you so much for Always We Begin Again," Fred wrote. "I love that little book, and had not known about it; and, of course, it means all the more to me because it came from you. Joanne and I thank you for your blessed friendship all through the years. Love to all the Madigans. Gratefully, Fred."

A few days later, I received another parcel from Pittsburgh, this one containing a little book with a mirror on the cover. It was called *You Are Special: Neighborly Wisdom from Mister Rogers.*

"Dear Tim," he wrote in the inscription. "You are special. Always have been. Always will be!! Grateful for your lifelong friendship. Fred."

But he never mentioned to me his own ordeal. On New Year's Day, Catherine saw Fred on television as the grand marshal of the Rose Bowl Parade in California. She said he was smiling, but looked very thin.

There continued to be no reply to my e-mail messages of January. Though I still did not know the nature of Fred's problem, I knew it had to be something serious, and decided not to impose with a telephone call on what was obviously a very private time for Fred and his family.

Not until a day in mid-January did I begin to learn for certain of his illness. That day, Richard Kaufman, Fred's good friend and the composer of the Mister Rogers' Neighborhood symphony that was to premiere in Dallas, called me at the request of Fred's family. He told me about Fred's abdominal surgery, speaking also of bone scans and long stays in a Pittsburgh hospital. Though he could not say for certain it was cancer, Richard said that Fred's condition was obviously life-threatening, and that the family had chosen to keep his condition very private to avoid a media circus.

On a Sunday afternoon, January 19, Catherine, Patrick, and I drove to Dallas to hear Richard Kaufman's symphony. David Newell made the trip from Pittsburgh, representing Fred that afternoon as Mr. McFeely, the Speedy Delivery man. After the concert, I found David in the lobby of the Dallas concert hall.

"It's not good," he said.

In mid-February I could wait no longer. I dialed Fred's number in Pittsburgh from my desk at the newspaper and heard Joanne's weary voice at the other end of the line.

"I've been better," she said.

Yes, it was stomach cancer, she said, and the disease was very aggressive. Fred was under the care of hospice at their Pittsburgh apartment and did not have long to live. By then I had guessed as much. I asked Joanne if Fred was afraid.

"Not for himself," she said. "As you might expect, his only worry is for me and the rest of his family."

"'This isn't fair," I said. "He's always taken such good care of himself. The world still needs him so much."

"I know, Tim," she said. "There are some things we will never understand."

I desperately wanted to speak to Fred myself, and nearly asked Joanne if I could say just a few words to him on the telephone. But I ultimately decided not to.

"If the opportunity presents itself," I said to Joanne, "please tell Fred that I love him."

"The opportunity has already presented itself," she said. "And it will again."

That same day, not long after I hung up with Joanne, Fred's friend and colleague Bill Isler called from Pittsburgh with a more detailed description of Fred's illness, which he said had first been diagnosed in November.

"We're reaching out to a very short list of people," Bill said. "And you're on that list."

"Please say good-bye to him for me," I said.

"I will," Bill said. "You can be sure of that."

I hung up the telephone and spent the next four hours driving alone in the rural hills of North Texas, with sad music playing in my car, nearly blinded at times by the tears. On the morning of February 27, my wife came across the news on the Internet. She was weeping when she came into the living room of our home, where I was sipping my first cup of coffee.

"Fred died last night," she said.

My parents were visiting from Minnesota at the time, and we spent much of the day speaking of Fred, remembering his love and support when my brother was sick. We talked of the morning not long before Steve's death when the two of them spoke on the telephone. When Fred mentioned his wish to meet him, Steve had replied that their meeting would probably have to be in heaven. Who could have foretold that their heavenly acquaintance would come so soon?

That night on Nightline, Ted Koppel called Fred a "genius" and a "gentle giant." The following morning, his death was front-page news in virtually every paper in the country, coverage normally reserved for the deaths of presidents and popes. On February 28, my own essay was published on the front page of the *Star-Telegram*, which recalled my first trip to Pittsburgh; Fred's grief over the loss of Jim Stumbaugh; the first IPOY letter written to me in the midst of the Furies; the way Fred supported Steve and our family through my brother's illness and death.

"Now Fred is gone and my heart is broken," I wrote that day. "I hoard my memories of Fred Rogers, trying to recall every moment we spent together, every letter, every e-mail. Among those memories was this, something he told me a short time after my brother died. I remember that familiar awe in his voice. There is such a thin veil between this life and whatever comes after it,' Fred said then.

"It's very hard to believe that Fred himself has passed through the veil. Go peaceably into the mystery my dear, dear man. Go with God."

The next day, I was inundated with telephone calls and e-mail messages from readers who wanted to share their own memories of Mister Rogers. Many also offered words of consolation to me, which were gifts beyond measure. The note from one mother writing from a small town near Fort Worth was particularly beautiful.

First of all, allow me to express my deepest and heartfelt condolences to you on the loss of such an incredible friend—indeed, God-given guide—in your life. Fred Rogers was a neighbor to all of us who watched his show (and as a stay-at-home mom with two sons, I watched him twice a day for at least a decade). In your magnificent tribute to him, you have confirmed what I always suspected: that Fred Rogers' friendship would be almost unbearably sweet to know.

Secondly, allow me to thank you for sharing with pure honesty your struggle with The Furies and Fred's encouragement and love. Whether you intended to or not, you have spread his healing words to others who can use them, as I will for my seventeen-year-old son who struggles with suicidal depression and obsessive-compulsive disorder. My son survived a harrowing birth and brain damage, yet, even as I see him as my own miracle and gift from God, Andrew wrestles with why he has been left with so many struggles. I intend to commit Fred Rogers' words to memory and apply as needed!

I believe you wrote a wonderful tribute to Fred Rogers, but you did much, much more: you spread Fred's words and heart and faith like seed. And that seed will feed the spiritually hungry, and plant faith among those who are broken or in pain. You could not have given Fred Rogers a more fitting farewell and I, for one, know he's never been prouder of you.

Again, thank you for sharing so much, so lovingly, even as you grieve. May your memories of Fred Rogers bring you the comfort you deserve.

Bravo,

Susan Karnes

Aledo, Texas

As I read her note, I sat at my newspaper desk and quietly wept.

163

More than a year later, on another family vacation to Michigan, I made the drive east, entering the long tunnel in the small mountain to see downtown Pittsburgh explode into view on the far side, and, farther into the city, the majestic Cathedral of Learning, at Pitt. I rode the elevator to the second floor of the public television station and saw the door of Fred's office firmly closed and locked. Bill Isler and I walked down the street for lunch, reminiscing about Fred, marveling at our mutual good fortune to have experienced his epic goodness firsthand.

That afternoon I made the short drive to Latrobe, where I met another of Fred's closest friends, Father Douglas Nowicki, the archabbot at St. Vincent's Benedictine Monastery, in that small Pennsylvania city where Fred grew up. Douglas, who had known Fred well for decades, drove me past the large brick dwelling that had been Fred's childhood home, and other Latrobe places that had been special to him as a child. That night at dinner, Douglas and I also spoke of Fred's human greatness, agreeing that it was on the order of spiritual icons like Mother Teresa, Pope John Paul II, and the Dalai Lama.

"He would never use these words to describe himself, of course," Douglas said at dinner that night. "But Fred used to say of people like that, 'they were in touch with the eternal.' Fred was in touch with the eternal."

The next morning, I followed winding roads to a small country cemetery near Latrobe, then inched past ancient tombstones on a yellow brick road until the road came to an end. There, on top of a hill, sat the large white mausoleum. I peered through the glass and read Fred's name on the place he had been laid to rest, near the remains of several other family members. But I did not speak to Fred that day at his grave, did not pray, did not weep—because I knew that my friend was not there. He had gone somewhere else—just the other side of the thin veil, residing there with my brother Steve and all the saints. And from that side of the veil I knew I would always be able to hear him whisper to me in the moments when I needed to hear it most, "IPOY, my friend. IPOY."

On that warm, sunny morning, I smiled and looked through the mausoleum glass one last time before walking back to my car. Then I inched back down the yellow brick road, and drove off toward Pittsburgh, headed back to a very happy life.

Afterword

On an October day in 2006, Kory Kelly set off into the wilds of northern Minnesota, bird-hunting with a golden retriever named Sammy. When Kory did not return home as expected, hundreds of volunteers joined a ground and air search. Sammy turned up unharmed, but Kory's body was not located until the snow melted the following spring. Authorities speculated that he had gotten lost and froze to death. He was thirty-eight years old.

Kory and his family were members at Trinity Lutheran Church in my hometown of Crookston. They always attended the early service at 7:45 a.m., sitting a few rows from the front on the right-hand side. For obvious reasons, they had not been in their pew for the first two Sundays after Kory's tragic disappearance, which had been big news across the Upper Midwest.

On the third Sunday, I was visiting from Texas, seated with my friend, Marshall Olson, at the front of the church. It would be my privilege that morning to take the pulpit and share the story of my friendship with Fred Rogers, and the dark and tragic times through which Fred had tided me. Just before the early service began, Marshall whispered in my ear.

"The Kelly's are back," he said, referring to the large family filing in, Kory's mother and father, siblings, nieces and nephews.

I felt a moment of panic. How could I talk about my own painful journey in front of people who were already suffering so terribly? Alas, I had only one story to tell. That day in church, I spoke of my own despondence and pain and Fred's gentle and unwavering companionship through it. I talked of my brother's terminal illness, and how in that telephone conversation between Fred and Steve, Mister Rogers asked my brother to pray for him, because anyone who had suffered as Steve had suffered must be extremely close to God.

When the service was finished, I headed to the church basement, sitting to sign copies of *I'm Proud of You* for a line of people, many of whom had been my friends and neighbors. Eventually I heard a woman's voice above me.

"Mr. Madigan," she began, "I just want you to know that I'll be praying for Fred Rogers today."

I looked up. It was Kory Kelly's mother, Jan. I had not known her before, but that did not matter. I stood and took her in my arms. She was crying. I was crying. Everyone around us was crying. I will always remember that moment as one of the most grace-filled of my life. When I spoke to her about it two years later, Jan said she felt much the same way.

I marvel at it still. In a telephone conversation with my dying brother in 2000, Fred asks Steve to pray for him, thereby planting a seed that bears fruit in such a profound way in a Lutheran church basement in Minnesota six years later. But Fred was historically adept at brokering such things. I have come to believe Fred planted those seeds with every moment of his sacred presence and compassion, innumerable beginnings of love and goodness that continue to flower so widely in our suffering world today.

In the years after *I'm Proud of You* was published, I was frequently reminded of Fred's words to me when I was at my own lowest ebb: "I'm convinced fewer and fewer can escape major suffering in this life. The kingdom of God is for the broken hearted."

Many of the hundreds of emails I have received were from people in the throes of depression, or who were attempting to repair broken relationships, or had loved ones suffering from terminal illnesses, or mourned those who had already passed across "the thin veil between this life and whatever comes after it."

Several of their notes went something like this: "Tim, I know Fred wrote those letters to you, but it felt like they were written to me, too." If only those people knew how literally that was true. Fred was writing to everyone. I was just the unlikely middleman. "Your place in this life is unique, absolutely unique," he wrote. "Do you know how special you really are?" Fred would have said that same thing, and often did, to anyone who crossed his path in life. And he would have meant those words from the core of his being.

I also met those suffering people at every stop during my travels with the book. One afternoon at an appearance at a bookstore in Pittsburgh, I noticed a young woman sitting in the back of the audience, quietly weeping as I told my story. Later, she waited until I had finished signing books, so we could talk in private. She told me that earlier that same day she had completed her graduate work at the University of Pittsburgh. I was surprised that she chose to spend such a celebratory day with me in a bookstore.

"My father never has told me he was proud of me," she said, weeping again. Then it made more sense.

It was common for wives, mothers, sisters, girlfriends, to ask me to sign books for the men in their lives, guys who were going through their own versions of the Furies, but could not bring themselves to talk about it. I often felt that the book was written specifically for them, for men like me.

"From one guy to another," I generally wrote.

After a lecture at Barton College in North Carolina, a young man lingered until I was getting ready to leave.

"I have a question," he said. "I was always told that as a man, you were showing strength by keeping your troubles to yourself, by dealing with them alone. You mean that's not true?"

I assured him that in my experience that was crap, to put it politely.

"I think a man shows much more courage by being honest with his fears and feelings, sharing them with someone he can trust," I said.

The young man seemed relieved.

Finally, I have heard again and again from people who wanted to tell me about a "Mister Rogers in my life," a mentor, friend, or parent who had Fred's amazing knack for presence, who never judged, who always listened from the heart. Turns out those people are not as rare as we would think.

As I write this, it's been nearly a decade since Fred's death, six years since *I'm Proud of You* was first published. Catherine and I just celebrated twenty-two years of marriage. At our anniversary dinner, we marveled at our journey together. We also talked about a deepening understanding of what love in a marriage really is. Melanie and Patrick are grown, both of them very fine people of whom their mother and I are wildly proud.

I continue to have opportunities to tell the story of my friendship with Fred at places around the nation. A particularly memorable evening came in the fall of 2011, at an event hosted by WJCT, the public television station in Jacksonville, Florida. The question posed that night by WJCT President Michael Boylan was a new one. Michael had listened to me describe my relationship with my dad.

"If we were to talk to your children, what would they say about you as a father?"

I was momentarily speechless.

"That's not fair," I replied to some laughter from the audience.

There was another pause. Both Melanie and Patrick bear their share of wounds, many of which I know I inflicted.

"I think they would say I did the best I could," I finally answered that night in Florida.

Before *I'm Proud of You* was published, I was deeply concerned that my parents, especially my dad, would find parts of the book hurtful. But I felt I had no choice but to write honestly about my wounds, and what I saw as their origins in the relationship with him. I remember sending the manuscript to them in the spring of 2006 and holding my breath. My heart was hammering into my ribs when my mother called after finishing. I'll never forget the relief when she talked about how moving she thought it was. While he read it, my dad turned to my mom and asked this question: "I didn't beat him, did I?" But he got it, too. The book was about suffering human beings who did their best, a family that loved deeply despite wounds and imperfections common to almost everyone.

On a beautiful late-summer evening in 2006, a crowd of about three hundred came to a church sanctuary in the Twin Cities for one of my first lectures about the book. Many Minnesota friends were there that night, as were my parents (just a few weeks shy of their fiftieth wedding anniversary), brothers and sisters, nieces and nephews, who were seated together in the front pew. I began the talk this way:

"In our world, the movie stars and pro athletes tend to get the headlines and the standing ovations, while the real heroes of life, people who quietly go about their lives, raising their families, working hard, being faithful to their spouses—those people are pretty much ignored," I said. "But for one night, I'd like to change that. Tonight, I'd ask you to stand up and give my father a standing ovation, honoring him and the millions of other men like him who are the quiet heroes of our world, who just get up every morning and do the right thing."

The audience stood and the place erupted. My dad stood himself, turned toward the crowd and waved, then waved again. I'm very happy to report that when my dad got his moment, he milked it. Afterwards, I asked him what he thought.

"Well," he said. "I've never had a standing ovation before."

By that night, his mind was in the beginning stages of failing him; the terrible disease of Alzheimer's had begun to take its horrible and inexorable course. Eventually, he and my mother moved into the home of my sister, Terri, and her family. She and my mother became Dad's caregivers, heartbreaking and exhausting duty that became more difficult by the day.

Everything you needed to know about my dad you could learn by watching how those two women took care of him. Mom and Terri are extraordinary humans, to be sure, but my dad inspired that kind of devotion.

On one of my regular visits home, in December of 2009, I found dad weakened from pneumonia, his moments of lucidity more and more infrequent. On a Saturday morning, I helped get him into the shower, helped him with a bar of soap, and I don't know that there has ever been a time in my life when my heart was so full of love. Later on that same morning, I sat down close to Dad in his living room, within a few inches of his face so I could hear him if he spoke. Outside, huge snowflakes fell on a silent and beautiful Minnesota winter morning. Dad looked at me and his eyes moistened.

"May God bless you," he said.

Then he was gone, back into the recesses of his disease. But in that moment, in that one look, in those few words, the heavens parted for me. I felt I had received the benediction from my father that I had craved for so long. I wept that morning during the long walk to a Starbucks in St. Paul, and wept again on the walk home. I thought of Fred Rogers and my desperate letters to him in 1996. I remembered Fred's love and unconditional support for me then, but also how his compassion extended immediately to my father. With that compassion, Fred had planted yet another seed, one that had flowered on that snowy winter morning. On my next trip home a few months later, my father didn't recognize me at all. That didn't matter. I recognized him.

In June of 2011, there was another bout with pneumonia. The family gathered at Dad's bedside, praying the rosary and singing "For He's a Jolly Good Fellow." On June 12, a Sunday night, I lay down with him, and held his hand, listening to his labored breathing. I told him how much I loved him. The next morning I kissed him goodbye. A few hours later, while I was thirty thousand feet above the earth on my flight back to Texas, he joined Fred and Steve on the other side of the thin veil.

An Informal Bibliography

As I've written, on the wall of Fred's office was this phrase from *The Little Prince*, by Antoine de Saint-Exupery: "Inessential est invisible pour les yeux." (What is essential is invisible to the eye.) That "essential invisible" was, in one way or another, the topic of nearly everything my friend read, and he read prodigiously.

I'm grateful that many of those books came to be important to our friendship, beginning on my first visit to Pittsburgh in 1995, when I saw the Saint-Exupery quotation on Fred's wall, and learned for the first time of Fred's admiration for the Catholic writer Henri Nouwen.

What follows is a brief listing of some of the books we talked about, beginning with the works of Nouwen. The books that described the final chapters of his life were what Fred and I most often discussed. They included *The Return of the Prodigal Son, A Story of Homecoming; The Wounded Healer, Can You Drink the Cup?; Seeds of Hope: A Henri Nouwen Reader; Sabbatical Journey: The Diary of His Final Year; The Road To Daybreak: A Spiritual Journey;* and *The Inner Voice of Love: A Journey Through Anguish to Freedom.*

Fred also introduced me to the work of Frederick Buechner, a critically acclaimed novelist and ordained Christian minister who explored the mysteries of the spirit in singularly lovely prose. Buechner's *Listening to Your Life: Daily Meditations with Frederick Buechner* became one of my daily staples. Fred and I were great admirers of Thomas Merton, the famous Catholic monk and prolific author who died in 1968. My Merton favorites: *No Man Is an Island; Zen and the Birds of Appetite,* and *The Asian Journal of Thomas Merton.*

Among lay writers, *The Cloister Walk,* by Kathleen Norris, and *Traveling Mercies; Some Thoughts on Faith,* by Anne Lamott are two books read and wholly appreciated by us both.

As I've written, it was Fred who sent me *Tuesdays with Morrie; An Old Man, a Young Man, and Life's Greatest Lesson,* Mitch Albom's classic about his relationship with the dying professor, Morrie Schwartz. For Christmas 2002, I sent Fred a copy of *Always We Begin Again; The Benedictine Way of Living,* by a lawyer named John McQuiston II. That book was my last correspondence with Fred. It is comforting to think that, as Fred's fatal illness progressed, he might have been comforted at least a little by the simple beauty and humility of McQuiston's words.

From Readers

I truly feel that your writing was a "God sighting" for me. I struggle with looking for someone to accept me just as I am and be proud of me, too. I identified with so many of the themes of your book from the unconditional love of a friend, to the cancer death of your dear brother, to the "furies" that came close to ruining your marriage, to the simple love of Mountain Dew. . . . Suffice it to say that I laughed, cried, felt pride, felt pain, and without a doubt saw the love of your family, friends, and the Lord.

Kim Jessen

. . . [T]his has blessed me more than I could adequately share with you. I began the book last night and could not put it down. I found myself blinking back tears, yet vaulted to the most joyful heights, as I digested the pages of your spectacular brotherhood with Mr. Rogers. . . . You have left your mark on my life as profoundly as Mr. Rogers did all those years ago on television.

IPOY, indeed. Jyll Richburg, Tyler, Texas

What a remarkable book you've written. I took your book with me on a recent ride into Boston near a place called Public Gardens and also overlooking Boston Harbor. Well, I sat reading a few chapters—near the end of the book and was weeping—faucet on full blast. My, that makes me feel human.

You've touched a nerve. . . . Time to re-connect with my brothers. . . .

Scott M. Allen

Roslindale, Massachusetts

My sister died this past December from cancer. Your chapters about your brother's illness and death were so resonant and so cathartic. I have struggled with my faith in the past few months and consider it a gift from God that your book came into my hands. Sometimes someone else's journey can light the way.

Susan W.

.... I believe reading about your brother's passing helped me to shed tears about ones I have lost, and have not realized that the pain and grief was still inside of me. Thank you for sharing your experiences, your life, your family, your relationship with Fred. . . .

De Guggenheim

Houston

I sobbed for the two some odd hours it took to read IPOY to the end. I'm still working through all the wounded places of my life that have been blessed by the story of your journey. . . . Thank you again for sharing the grace of your friendships with Fred and Steve. . . . Thank you too, for ministering to me.

Andy Parker, Oceanside, California

How quickly I related to the fractured relationship and subsequent healing you experienced with your dad.

Joseph K. Schamburg
Illinois

I wanted to thank you for your message about healing in the family. As a Catholic priest, I am ushered into many difficult situations encountered by families. Your insights gave me so much to think and pray about. Sharing your insights in the context of your friendship with Mister Rogers makes your message so available and non-threatening. I believe you have contributed an important gift in your story. Thanks much for letting me in!

John Fraser

Your book has been a source of great healing for me and my . . . marriage. I've also been "finding" myself again, after 22 years of being lost inside since my father's suicide . . . self discovery ... all thanks to your book! I see so much of myself and my family in your book, from the days of my youth growing up in a small town, to my recent mental and marriage problems. . . . Tim, all I can say is THANK YOU for sharing your wonderful stories and . . . IPOY!

Peter
Twin Cities

Thank you from the bottom of my heart so much for your book. I cried through most of it and it touched my heart more than any book I have read. I feel like I knew your brother. I am going through a painful separation and my family is so very fractured. It is the most painful experience I have ever imagined and have had many days I wanted to quit living. For some reason, your book was a salvation to me. Thank you so much.

Cindy K.

Louisville, Kentucky

I could not sleep until I had written you. I just finished reading it and find myself sobbing and laughing all at the same time as I remember all that Mr. Rogers meant to me. . . . You have touched me with your words in ways you will never know. It is almost as if those letters you have hidden away are partly mine, that somehow Fred wrote them not just to you but to me, to all of us.

Karla Neese

Edmond, Oklahoma

My dad has never told me he is proud of me. Nor has he ever told me he loves me. What a great book you wrote—I wanted to THANK YOU for writing it. Have been so sad and depressed for the past couple years. A shrink told me to read your book. I read it, and then I sent it to my dad. The following is his response, a direct result of his reading your book. Thank you for writing the book. It has been the only thing that has started to mend a huge divide. I cannot thank you enough. God Bless you, and God Bless Mr. Rogers!

IPOY

Sincerely,

Tom Landis, Dallas

Tom:

IPOY. I found things in the book that made me reflect on a number of things.

We all do things we regret. There are many things in life I would do differently and wish that they could be undone. Many things are done to us. The best we can really do is to forgive and move on. When you are feeling better I hope we can talk. It will be good for both of us.

Love, Dad

Your writing stirred up a lot of feelings of affirmation as well as gentle melancholy. At a time when the world craves shallow celebrity, your story touches some very deep, satisfying chords of friendship and faithfulness. Thanks.

Paul B. Seaton

Wayne, Pennsylvania

This book was a major inspiration for me and I thank you for putting yourself in it with a full heart.

Rabbi Neil Fleischmann

Your account of losing your brother simply ripped me up. I also lost a brother just a year younger than me when I was 21. Your honesty about such a loss is something I have never been able to grasp in my own moments of journaling, and I commend you for digging so deep. . . . Thank you. That's really all I have to say.

Joy Underhill

I have renewed it from the library twice because I am reluctant to let it go. I got it to read at rest time at the after school program where I work with a child with autism. You brought me to tears so often that I had to finish it at home. Honesty such as yours is rare and an enormous gift.

Denie L. Hayden

You caused this fat monk to sob uncontrollably. As I read the death watch you kept with your brother, I was transported to the deathbed of my mother. The emotions you brought forth were wonderfully painful. . . . Thank you for writing such a beautiful book and for sharing such a wonderful friendship.

Fr. Jerome Machar

Abbey of Genesee

I can't remember a book that has inspired me more. I used to love watching Mr. Rogers with my children about twenty years ago. God bless you for this writing. You have made the world brighter for all who are touched by it. I will never be the same and will share this. I already have. Diane Hornbeck

Savannah, Georgia

As a home health social worker and Coroner's Assistant, I had come to fear that my decades of extending myself into the heart and souls of others had taken the most costly toll—a deflating of my heart in my middle years. But alas, I have been rescued, the tears are flowing again. . . . God has used your book to soften my heart, to remind me of my calling, to remind me of the beautiful gift that God affords us when we exist in empathy with others. And to think I was just blaming this on menopause! . . . Your family is to be cherished for publicly sharing the path that you shared with Steve. Your example will not soon be forgotten.

Luann Davidson

I tell you what, I can't wait to see Mr. Rogers in heaven and give him a hug. I loved him before I read your book. Now I truly cherish all of my memories of watching his show. God Bless you. I believe God had me read your book for many reasons. You and Mr. Rogers have blessed me. Sincerely, Allison

Proud mother of three

About the Author

Tim Madigan is an award-winning newspaper journalist and the author of two critically acclaimed books; *See No Evil: Blind Devotion and Bloodshed in David Koresh's Holy War* and *The Burning: Massacre, Destruction, and the Tulsa Race Riot of 1921.* He lives in Arlington, Texas, with his wife, Catherine. They have two adult children.

For more information about the author, visit www.timmadigan.com or find him on Twitter at @tsmadigan or @MrRogers_said

Front cover design by Mark Hoffer

Made in the USA
Middletown, DE
18 April 2015